Case Studies *for* School Leaders

Case Studies for School Leaders

Implementing the ISLLC Standards

William L. Sharp
James K. Walter
Helen M. Sharp

A SCARECROWEDUCATION BOOK

The Scarecrow Press, Inc.
Lanham, Maryland, and Oxford
1999
Originally published by
Technomic Publishing Co, Inc.
Lancaster, Pennsylvania

A SCARECROWEDUCATION BOOK

Published in the United States of America
by Scarecrow Press, Inc.
A Member of the Rowman & Littlefield Publishing Group
4720 Boston Way, Lanham, Maryland 20706
www.scarecroweducation.com

12 Hid's Copse Road
Cumnor Hill, Oxford OX2 9JJ, England

The Technomic edition of this book was catalogued as follows by the Library
of Congress:
Main entry under title:
    Case Studies for School Leaders: Implementing the ISLLC Standards
Bibliography: p.
Includes index p. 249
Library of Congress Catalog Card No. 97-62077
ISBN No. 1-56676-608-7
Reprinted by ScarecrowEducation

⊖™ The paper used in this publication meets the minimum requirements of
American National Standard for Information Sciences—Permanence of
Paper for Printed Library Materials, ANSI/NISO Z39.48–1992.
Manufactured in the United States of America.

Table of Contents

v

5. Standard 3 Case Studies   105

6. Standard 4 Case Studies   165

Foreword

After some false starts, the field of educational leadership finally is maturing to become a full-fledged profession. At the core of all major professions is agreement on a common base of knowledge and performance required for admission to practice. While the individual states administer actual licensure procedures for the various professions, they do so based on core standards established across states by these professions.

The development of "Standards for School Leaders," published in late 1996 by the Interstate School Leaders Licensure Consortium (ISLLC) provides for the first time a common base of knowledge and performances for school leaders in the 24 states representing the Consortium. Other states will likely join the Consortium as the advantages of common standards are understood. All other major licensed professions have attained this status of common standards some decades ago.

While the ISLLC Standards include knowledge, performance, and dispositions, the clear focus is on performance. Leadership is active, not passive. John Gardner defines leadership as "judgment in action." Leaders must not only understand, they must act according to that understanding. Leaders must not only be disposed in certain ways, they must act on those dispositions. Performance, therefore, is the integrating element in the profession of educational leadership. Performance ties knowledge and disposition together in action. Performance reflects both understanding and inclination. Without performance, leadership becomes passive, even insipid. With performance, leadership causes change and shapes events.

If performance is the paramount reflection of educational leadership, if it defines what leaders actually must know and do, then it follows that programs preparing educational leaders should focus on helping students to apply their knowledge and exhibit their dispositions in a performance framework. Or, to state it more directly, preparation programs need to provide an extensive menu of venues that provide opportunities to perform, including an evaluation of these performances. Typical approaches to offering these learning opportunities include various clinical methodologies incorporating simulations, role-plays, case studies, practica, internships and portfolios, sometimes with technologies as sophisticated as virtual reality.

We now have two decades of research with practicing school leaders that confirm the relative value of performance methodologies as compared to passive methodologies. Most recently, a 1996 study by Sharp and Walter reaffirms the views of experienced school leaders that traditional coursework trails far behind internships and other performance-related methodologies when applied to the new ISLLC Standards. Most of the new Standards will not be achieved in a traditional college classroom, according to experienced principals and other educational administrators.

Given these realities, a case study publication based on the new ISLLC Standards provides a valuable resource for instructors who wish to shape their educational leadership program with a performance curriculum that addresses these new Interstate Standards. Students, also, likely will appreciate a reference organized on ISLLC material since these Standards possess credibility based on their broad and thorough development, and since the Standards will directly affect licensure requirements in a growing number of states.

As educational leadership emerges into a progressive, fullfledged profession, key changes are required in preparation programs. This book of case studies will provide a useful resource for persons attending to those important program changes.

Scott D. Thomson
Executive Secretary
National Policy Board for
Educational Administration

Preface

The Interstate School Leaders Licensure Consortium document, "Standards for School Leaders," marks an abrupt departure from the traditional textbook containing chapters on budgeting, personnel management, facilities, organization patterns, etc. These Standards specify precise behavior—called Performances—that educational leaders need to be successful. As Scott Thomson states in the Foreword, there is a common base of knowledge and performance, and the methodologies that must be used for training are performance ones, not passive methodologies.

This book of case studies in educational administration is intended to promote the idea that practicing administrators need to be reflective administrators. While there is the tendency to feel that administrators must, due to time constraints, always operate in a reactive mode, we feel that they need to study scenarios that provoke thought and generate discussion of the problems and issues that face them in schools today. The book includes many different topics as well as groups that administrators encounter, including other administrators, parents, community groups, students, and other school personnel. All of the 133 case studies are based on the 96 Performance Objectives stated in the "Standards for School Leaders."

The case studies can be used by people preparing to become educational leaders and by current practicing administrators. What can result, hopefully, is some degree of preparedness, using this common set of Performances across the states. Most of these case studies actually occurred, putting some school leaders on the spot when they did. We feel that this book can be valuable in several ways:

- Each case study provides a way of thinking about the six Standards and the Performance Objectives required to fulfill them.
- Each case study further explains an individual Performance Objective with a specific real-life example.
- Each case study represents a challenge, demanding not only understanding but also a reaction or a response and, possibly, the basis for some action to take in the leader's school now, if needed.
- Each case study can be a guide to potential problems a school leader might encounter in trying to achieve such high expectations.

Specifically, while the book is useful for some practicing administrators, it is anticipated that its major use will be in (1) administrator preparation programs and (2) state leadership development programs. This book of Case Studies can be used alongside traditional textbooks in educational administration graduate preparation programs for courses like Introduction to Administration, The Principalship, and The Superintendency. Also, as preparation programs change to more non-traditional methods to emphasize active, performance-based leadership training and reflection, this case study book can be used as a centerpiece in the program.

This book can also be used in those states that are establishing training academies or leadership development programs for administrators. These state programs require exercises for the further training of current administrators and assessment tools for future administrators who are in the programs. These programs often require students to read case studies about issues in schools and answer questions like the following:

- What should the administrator do next?
- What factors should this administrator consider before responding?
- Who should the administrator consult before making a decision?
- What are the consequences of the administrator's action?

This book of case studies is designed to do just that—to present 133 examples of what can and does confront school leaders, and then to ask the reader questions like those just mentioned.

It is hoped that the case studies in this book can contribute to the reflective, performance-based training that future school leaders will need.

Acknowledgements

The authors would like to thank the Interstate School Leaders Licensure Consortium for the use of their Standards for School Leaders in this book. Neil Shipman served as Director of the Consortium, and Joseph Murphy was Chair of the Consortium. We would also like to thank Scott D. Thomson for his help and suggestions at the beginning of the project and for his writing of the Foreword. At Technomic Publishing, Joseph Eckenrode and Susan Farmer were very helpful with their suggestions during the writing of the book, and the authors appreciate their encouraging us during the project. Dr. Walter would like to thank C. Yvette Wilmoth for her typing of his portion of the book. We would both like to thank Helen M. Sharp, who not only contributed many of the case studies but also edited the manuscript thoroughly for us.

WILLIAM L. SHARP

CHAPTER 1

Introduction

An Explanation of the Standards and Indicators

This book contains 133 individual case studies, based on six Standards and 96 Performance Indicators developed by the Interstate School Leaders Licensure Consortium (ISLLC). One of the purposes of this Consortium was to establish a "common set of standards that would apply to nearly all formal leadership positions in education, not just principals."[1] In establishing these Standards and Performances, ISLLC considered and relied on the "research on the linkages between educational leadership and productive schools" and the "significant trends in society and education that hold implications for emerging views of leadership." The Consortium acknowledged that the social fabric of our nation has been changing and that we are a more diverse nation in many ways, requiring new types of leadership in our schools. In addition, the members of this group felt that "stakeholders external to the school building—parents, interested members of the corporate sector and leaders in the community—will increasingly play significantly enhanced roles in education." The authors of this book agreed— hence many of the case studies involve parents and community members.

The Consortium stated that there was "a major void in this area of educational administration—a set of common standards remains conspicuous by its absence." Hopefully, the ISLLC Standards will

[1]All quotations in this chapter are taken from *Interstate School Leaders Licensure Consortium: Standards for School Leaders.* 1996. Washington, DC: Council of Chief State School Officers, pp. 5–7.

help fill this void, and the 133 case studies in this book will help make these Standards come alive to school administrators.

The Evolution of the Project to Write the Standards

In August, 1994, the Council of Chief State School Officers formed the Interstate School Leaders Licensure Consortium. One of the purposes of the group was to develop these common Standards and assessments for licensing principals and other school leaders for admission to practice. Funded by The Pew Charitable Trusts and the Danforth Foundation, 24 states contributed to the project as well as 11 professional associations. Neil Shipman served as Director of the Consortium, with Joseph Murphy of Vanderbilt as Chairperson. The representatives of the member states and the professional associations spent two years discussing and developing the Standards and indicators, using research, the knowledge of the representatives, and advice from people in public schools and universities. After many drafts and revisions, the Standards for School Leaders document was adopted by the full Consortium on November 2, 1996.

The Relationship between the Standards and This Book

The document adopted by the Consortium contains six Standards for School Leaders. Each Standard is assigned to a different chapter in this book, Chapters 3–8. The Consortium document then lists, for each of the six Standards, a number of items under the headlines of Knowledge, Dispositions, and Performances. Our book is only concerned with the Performances section. We called each of these a Performance Objective. There are 96 Performance Objectives for the six Standards, and the book contains 133 case studies, all based on these 96 Performance Objectives. The Performance Objective(s) for each case study is listed immediately before the case study numbered subhead. In addition to showing case studies by Standard and Performance Objective, an Index in the back of the book lists case studies by topic.

A List of the Standards and Performance Objectives

Below is a complete list of the six Standards for School Leaders and the 96 Performance Objectives. These are repeated in the appropriate chapter (3–8).

Standard 1

A school administrator is an educational leader who promotes the success of all students by facilitating the development, articulation, implementation, and stewardship of a vision of learning that is shared and supported by the school community.

Performance Objectives for Standard 1

The administrator facilitates processes and engages in activities ensuring that

- The vision and mission of the school are effectively communicated to staff, parents, students, and community members.
- The vision and mission are communicated through the use of symbols, ceremonies, stories, and similar activities.
- The core beliefs of the school vision are modeled for all stakeholders.
- The vision is developed with and among stakeholders.
- The contributions of school community members to the realization of the vision are recognized and celebrated.
- Progress toward the vision and mission is communicated to all stakeholders.
- The school community is involved in school improvement efforts.
- The vision shapes the educational programs, plans, and actions.

- An implementation plan is developed in which objectives and strategies to achieve the vision and goals are clearly articulated.
- Assessment data related to student learning are used to develop the school vision and goals.
- Relevant demographic data pertaining to students and their families are used in developing the school mission and goals.
- Barriers to achieving the vision are identified, clarified, and addressed.
- Needed resources are sought and obtained to support the implementation of the school mission and goals.
- Existing resources are used in support of the school vision and goals.
- The vision, mission, and implementation plans are regularly monitored, evaluated, and revised.

Standard 2

A school administrator is an educational leader who promotes the success of all students by advocating, nurturing, and sustaining a school culture and instructional program conducive to student learning and staff professional growth.

Performance Objectives for Standard 2

The administrator facilitates processes and engages in activities ensuring that

- All individuals are treated with fairness, dignity, and respect.
- Professional development promotes a focus on student learning consistent with the school vision and goals.
- Students and staff feel valued and important.
- The responsibilities and contributions of each individual are acknowledged.
- Barriers to student learning are identified, clarified, and addressed.
- Diversity is considered in developing learning experiences.
- Lifelong learning is encouraged and modeled.

- There is a culture of high expectations for self, student, and staff performance.
- Technologies are used in teaching and learning.
- Student and staff accomplishments are recognized and celebrated.
- Multiple opportunities to learn are available to all students.
- The school is organized and aligned for success.
- Curricular, cocurricular, and extracurricular programs are designed, implemented, evaluated, and refined.
- Curriculum decisions are based on research, expertise of teachers, and the recommendations of learned societies.
- The school culture and climate are assessed on a regular basis.
- A variety of sources of information is used to make decisions.
- Student learning is assessed using a variety of techniques.
- Multiple sources of information regarding performance are used by staff and students.
- A variety of supervisory and evaluation models is employed.
- Pupil personnel programs are developed to meet the needs of students and their families.

Standard 3

A school administrator is an educational leader who promotes the success of all students by ensuring management of the organization, operations, and resources for a safe, efficient, and effective learning environment.

Performance Objectives for
Standard 3

The administrator facilitates processes and engages in activities ensuring that

- Knowledge of learning, teaching, and student development is used to inform management decisions.
- Operational procedures are designed and managed to maximize opportunities for successful learning.
- Emerging trends are recognized, studied, and applied as appropriate.

- Operational plans and procedures to achieve the vision and goals of the school are in place.
- Collective bargaining and other contractual agreements related to the school are effectively managed.
- The school plant, equipment, and support systems operate safely, efficiently, and effectively.
- Time is managed to maximize attainment of organizational goals.
- Potential problems and opportunities are identified.
- Problems are confronted and resolved in a timely manner.
- Financial, human, and material resources are aligned to the goals of schools.
- The school acts entrepreneurally to support continuous improvement.
- Organizational systems are regularly monitored and modified as needed.
- Stakeholders are involved in decisions affecting schools.
- Responsibility is shared to maximize ownership and accountability.
- Effective problem-framing and problem-solving skills are used.
- Effective conflict-resolution skills are used.
- Effective group-process and consensus-building skills are used.
- Effective communication skills are used.
- There is effective use of technology to manage school operations.
- Fiscal resources of the school are managed responsibly, efficiently, and effectively.
- A safe, clean, and aesthetically pleasing school environment is created and maintained.
- Human resource functions support the attainment of school goals.
- Confidentiality and privacy of school records are maintained.

Standard 4

A school administrator is an educational leader who promotes the success of all students by collaborating with families and community members, responding to diverse community interests and needs, and mobilizing community resources.

Performance Objectives for Standard 4

The administrator facilitates processes and engages in activities ensuring that

- High visibility, active involvement, and communication with the larger community is a priority.
- Relationships with community leaders are identified and nurtured.
- Information about family and community concerns, expectations, and needs is used regularly.
- There is outreach to different business, religious, political, and service agencies and organizations.
- Credence is given to individuals and groups whose values and opinions may conflict.
- The school and community serve one another as resources.
- Available community resources are secured to help the school solve problems and achieve goals.
- Partnerships are established with area businesses, institutions of higher education, and community groups to strengthen programs and support school goals.
- Community youth family services are integrated with school programs.
- Community stakeholders are treated equitably.
- Diversity is recognized and valued.
- Effective media relations are developed and maintained.
- A comprehensive program of community relations is established.
- Public resources and funds are used appropriately and wisely.
- Community collaboration is modeled for staff.
- Opportunities for staff to develop collaborative skills are provided.

Standard 5

A school administrator is an educational leader who promotes the success of all students by acting with integrity, fairness, and in an ethical manner.

Performance Objectives for
Standard 5

The administrator

- Examines personal and professional values.
- Demonstrates a personal and professional code of ethics.
- Demonstrates values, beliefs, and attitudes that inspire others to higher levels of performance.
- Serves as a role model.
- Accepts responsibility for school operations.
- Considers the impact of administrative practices on others.
- Uses the influence of the office to enhance the educational program rather than for personal gain.
- Treats people fairly, equitably, and with dignity and respect.
- Protects the rights and confidentiality of students and staff.
- Demonstrates appreciation for and sensitivity to the diversity in the school community.
- Recognizes and respects the legitimate authority of others.
- Examines and considers the prevailing values of the diverse school community.
- Expects that others in the school community will demonstrate integrity and exercise ethical behavior.
- Opens the school to public scrutiny.
- Fulfills legal and contractual obligations.
- Applies laws and procedures fairly, wisely, and considerately.

Standard 6

A school administrator is an educational leader who promotes the success of all students by understanding, responding to, and influencing the larger political, social, economic, legal, and cultural context.

Performance Objectives for
Standard 6

The administrator facilitates processes and engages in activities ensuring that

- The environment in which schools operate is influenced on behalf of students and their families.
- Communication occurs among the school community concerning trends, issues, and potential changes in the environment in which schools operate.
- There is ongoing dialogue with representatives of diverse community groups.
- The school community works within the framework of policies, laws, and regulations enacted by local, state, and federal authorities.
- Public policy is shaped to provide quality education for students.
- Lines of communication are developed with decision-makers outside the school community.

CHAPTER 2

Leadership Theory[2]

Introduction

Although most of this book is devoted to individual case studies about administrative situations, it is important to include a discussion of different leadership theories and styles. This chapter provides a theoretical background to the real-life experiences mentioned in the case studies that will follow. Sometimes school administrators (and students in our administration classes) say that they are interested in "practice" rather than "theory," that they do not want to hear about theory but want to know what to do in certain circumstances.

But it is important for administrators to have some knowledge about leadership theory and to have thought about their styles of leadership. This knowledge can give them a basis for making decisions when these situations arise. So, before we come to the "situations" in the form of case studies, here is a short discussion about leadership theory and leadership styles.

Considerable research has been done in the area of management, usually in business and industry. This has resulted in various theories and viewpoints. This chapter will examine those theories with the thought that an administrator's style of leadership may be based on one or more of these viewpoints. Since most readers of this book will have taken an administrative theory course, the examination of these theories will be relatively brief.

[2]This chapter is adapted, in part, with permission, from *The School Superintendent: The Profession and the Person,* by Sharp and Walter, also published by Technomic,© 1997.

Classical Organization Theory

This theory has two viewpoints: scientific management and administrative management. Scientific management was espoused by Frederick W. Taylor (1911), who looked at management from the viewpoint of the job of the individual workers. His four principles were as follows:

(1) Scientific job analysis—Each job should be examined to see what had to be done and to determine the "one best way" to do the job.
(2) Selection of personnel—The next step was to pick the right person to do the job and to train this employee to do the job in the "right" way.
(3) Management cooperation—Managers and employees should cooperate to see that the jobs are done as they should be done.
(4) Functional supervising—Managers should spend their time planning and organizing, while the employees should be doing the jobs for which they were hired.

While scientific management deals with the individual workers, the second view under the classical organization theory, administrative management, deals with the whole organization.

This theory, credited to Fayol (1949), Gulick and Uruick (1937), and Weber (1947), stated that all managers performed five basic functions: planning, organizing, commanding, coordinating, and controlling. Fayol felt that managers should exert authority and that the workers should be disciplined and obey these orders. The interests of the organization should take precedence over the interests of the individuals who worked for the organization. Also, the organization should have a definite chain of command with each person only reporting to one superior (pp. 20–41).

Others who studied management disagreed with the classical organization theory, feeling that it ignored the psychological needs of the workers as well as the need to motivate workers with something besides money. They felt that, for many workers, it was unrealistic to expect them to put the organization's needs ahead of their own interests. This led to the Human Relations Theory of management.

Human Relations Theory and
Behavioral Science Theory

Elton Mayo (1933) and Kurt Lewin (1939) felt that the human element must be taken into account. How employees worked together was important; how they felt about their jobs was important; morale was important. They theorized that groups that participated in decisions and were more democratic were more productive and that they achieved group goals better than groups under traditional authoritarian control.

The Behavioral Science Theory, to a large extent, combined both of these theories. Barnard (1938), along with Bakke (1955) and Argyris (1957), felt that the organization goals had to be met, and the goals of the employee had to be met as well. Managers had to have the technical skills to achieve the organizational goals, but they also had to have the human relations skills to help the workers achieve their own goals. It was felt that there was often an inherent conflict between the individual worker and the organization. Organizations often tried to repress the workers, causing frustration and indifference on the part of the employees. When people stayed within the same organization over time, their needs changed, and this should be recognized by the management.

This latter notion is certainly seen in schools. Teachers often have the identical classes (courses or grade levels), textbooks, and classrooms year after year. It is no wonder that they sometimes become frustrated and "burned out." That is why staff development is so important, not only for beginning teachers, but for those who have been at the same schools for years.

McGregor's Theories

Two famous theories were posed by McGregor (1960), Theory X and Theory Y. These theories were based on differing assumptions that managers might have about their employees.

In Theory X, managers feel that

- Workers dislike the work and will try to find ways to avoid the work when possible. They are lazy.

- Since they dislike work, employees must be supervised very closely and possibly threatened.
- Employees work better when they are directed and controlled by the manager. In fact, workers prefer this.

Theory Y, in contrast, states that the managers feel that

- Work is as natural as play or rest.
- Rewarding workers for achievement makes them more committed to the organizational goals.
- Workers accept and seek responsibility if they are treated properly.

Twenty years later, Ouchi (1981) developed Theory Z, based on Japanese business practices. This theory looked at the whole organization instead of only looking at it from the perspective of the manager, like Theories X and Y. Theory Z involves a long-term commitment to an organization and includes workers in decision-making, establishing individual responsibilities for the employees and the organization's commitment to the worker and his/her family.

In the school setting, Theory Z means shared decision-making, trust among all people in the school/district, motivating each other to seek a high quality of education for the students, and an understanding and acceptance of the objectives of the district by the employees. Teachers would see that working towards these objectives was in their own self-interest, and this would result in better productivity. Rewards under Theory Z are long-term, rather than short-time, a problem in schools where we typically have salary schedules that reward everyone equally, regardless of motivation or performance.

This brief review of management theories suggests that managers themselves are not single-minded. Just as there are different theories, there are different ways in which school administrators manage their jobs, supervise people, and work with superiors. Different leaders have different leadership styles. While some administrators are very autocratic, others are *laissez-faire*, and still others are democratic. Style probably depends somewhat on a manager's personality, prior experience, and how he/she was treated by former principals and superintendents. Yet behavior can change. Administrators with one style sometimes see a reason to develop another style, either by seeing others succeed with a particular style or because they feel they have not been as successful as they would like to be.

Of course, school administrators do not always use the same style all the time. For example, while superintendent Jones has a dominant style that is quite democratic, seeking the advice of her staff, she sometimes must make autocratic decisions.

Each administrator has to develop his/her own leadership style. And, this may change as the administrator moves from district to district or when the supervisor (or school board) dictates that the style must change. Regardless of the dominant style used, the administrator should understand that there are other styles and should know the advantages and disadvantages of each style.

The case studies in the remainder of this book suggest situations that may occur—in fact, many of these case studies have happened in the professional lives of the authors. It should be helpful for administrators to read these case studies, consider the discussion questions, and decide how they would have handled each situation. As administrators go through these case studies, it is hoped that they will think about their leadership styles and the theories that influence them.

References

Argyris, C. 1957. *Personality and Organization.* New York: Harper & Row.

Bakke, E. W. 1955. *The Fusion Process.* New Haven, CT: Yale Univ. Press.

Barnard, C. I. 1938. *The Functions of the Executive.* Cambridge, MA: Harvard Univ. Press.

Fayol, H. 1949. *General and Industrial Administration.* New York: Pitman (translated from the 1916 French edition).

Gulick, L. and L. Uruick, eds. 1937. *Papers on the Science of Administration.* New York: Columbia University Press.

Lewin, K., R. Lippitt, and R. White. 1939. "Patterns of Aggressive Behavior in Experimentally Created 'Social Climates,' " *Journal of Social Psychology,* 10, pp. 271-299.

Mayo, E. 1933. *The Human Problems of an Industrial Civilization.* New York: Macmillan.

McGregor, D. 1960. *The Human Side of Entreprise.* New York: McGraw-Hill.
Ouchi, W. G. 1981. *Theory Z: How American Business Can Meet the Japanese Challenge.* Reading, PA: Addison-Wesley.
Taylor, F. W. 1911. *Principles of Scientific Management.* New York: Harper.
Weber, M. 1947. *The Theory of Social and Economic Organization.* New York: Oxford University Press (English translation).

CHAPTER 3

Standard 1 Case Studies

A school administrator is an educational leader who promotes the success of all students by facilitating the development, articulation, implementation, and stewardship of a vision of learning that is shared and supported by the school community.

PERFORMANCE OBJECTIVE

THE ADMINISTRATOR FACILITATES
PROCESSES AND ENGAGES IN
ACTIVITIES ENSURING THAT
—The vision and mission of the school are
effectively communicated to staff, parents,
students, and community members.

Case Study 1

The last item on the administrative team agenda was "Explain the School's Mission." Mr. Andrews, the superintendent, asked his principals the following question: "How do you think each of you could best tell the staff and the community about the mission of your school?" Mr. Grove, from the elementary school, answered, "Well, I might try sending out a newsletter to the parents. I understand the school had one for a few years and then dropped it for some reason before I got here." Mr. Anderson, from the high school, said, "I have used a newsletter for a couple of years, but I really have not used it to tell what we were trying to accomplish. I used it more to tell parents when certain events were going to be held or to tell which colleges were visiting—that sort of thing."

Mrs. Long, the middle school principal, asked, "These newsletters could be used for parents, but should we send the same thing to the staff or send something else?"

Discussion Questions

1 What do you think about this idea of using school newsletters to convey the vision and the mission of the school? Are there other ways or better ways to do this?

2 Some schools have a school slogan that tells the school's mission. Do you know of any? How has this worked? Do you know your school's mission and, if so, can you think of an appropriate slogan?

3 What is a good way to communicate the school's mission to the staff? Have you seen good internal newsletters? Should the staff discuss this topic at meetings?

4 In what ways can school administrators communicate the school's mission to the community besides using written methods? Are there appropriate community meetings where this can be discussed?

5 Does the community care about the school's mission or is it more concerned with good grades, good athletic teams, and tax rates?

6 What obligation is there to communicate the mission to the students? Is this important? The "school's mission" does not sound like an interesting topic for students. How could you reword this?

PERFORMANCE OBJECTIVE

THE ADMINISTRATOR FACILITATES
PROCESSES AND ENGAGES IN
ACTIVITIES ENSURING THAT
—The vision and mission are communicated
  through the use of symbols, ceremonies,
  stories, and similar activities.

Case Study 2

When Jack Robinson became the principal of Nile River High School, he soon learned that both the staff and the students had low morale and lacked school spirit. "What can I do?" Jack asked his assistant principal. "I don't know, Jack," was the noncommittal reply.

The assistant, Hal Jones, had been in the district for 17 years and had been passed over by the superintendent for the position that Jack Robinson has assumed. At that point, Jack Robinson realized that whatever changes needed to be made would have to be his ultimate decision.

For several days, he thought about school spirit and the morale of the teachers. He knew there was little interaction among the staff, and there appeared to be total apathy as far as Nile River was concerned. His mission must be twofold: to bring up staff morale and to instill school spirit in the student body.

His plan was to establish some type of ceremony that the students would look forward to as potential upper upperclassmen and graduates. He contacted a ring manufacturer and discussed his ideas. Instead of allowing all students to purchase class rings, Robinson elected to have rings available only to juniors and seniors. The rings would be worn after a ceremony held in the auditorium of the school. The history and spirit of Nile River, as well as its mission and vision of learning for students, would be told to the underclassman. What he was attempting was to instill understanding of the importance of the school and its tradition through this impressive ceremony. He was hoping that this would become a new custom at Nile River.

As an interesting side light to this, Robinson found that after the ceremony several of the teachers commented about how impressed they were with both the ceremony and the student participation. Some went so far as to say that this was the first time they had been to any Nile River function and that they truly enjoyed it.

Discussion Questions

1 Do you think that Jack Robinson should have been told about the low morale and lack of spirit within the school community?

2 Did the principal exert too much top-down authority by arbitrarily mandating only juniors and seniors be allowed to wear the class rings?

3 Could the principal have involved other groups such as the teachers, the parents, and the students?

4 What would you have done if you came into a situation where an assistant was upset with being passed over for the job that you received?

5 Did the superintendent, through his personal style, add to the problems that affected the staff at Nile River?

6 Should Jack Robinson look at the problem of staff morale and the problem of low school spirit as two separate issues, or were they interrelated?

7 If the ring ceremony had not been successful, what other new ceremonies or traditions could have enhanced morale and school spirit?

PERFORMANCE OBJECTIVE

THE ADMINISTRATOR FACILITATES
PROCESSES AND ENGAGES IN
ACTIVITIES ENSURING THAT
—The vision and mission are communicated
through the use of symbols, ceremonies,
stories, and similar activities.

Case Study 3

"Our vision of learning for students includes academic excellence as well as their involvement in the school community and preparation for the future—further education and jobs," states the superintendent. "The mission here is, as it has always been, academic excellence." His comments occur while he is interviewing a candidate for the vacant principal's position. "I'm interested in your ideas about communicating the mission and vision to Central High School's professional staff and students," he encourages.

The candidate specifies ongoing activities directed toward students, including

- an all-school assembly featuring a motivational speaker who will challenge students to excel academically in view of the school's mission and to reach their full potential through involvement in all phases of school life

- an assembly featuring five or six successful Central graduates; each addresses the high school's most memorable traditions (for example, no one walks on the Central Flame insignia in front of the offices, and seniors clean, polish, and "guard" the school seal). Then, each speaker explains Central's importance in his or her life and successes, including anecdotes about the school's milestones (national recognition for debate and oratory).
- a year's-end assembly recognizing students' progress and achievements, with prizes such as gift certificates, movie passes, and amusement park tickets—The focus is on perfect attendance, school and community service, no tardies in any class, outstanding homework records, and similar accomplishments.
- a weekend barbecue or picnic to start the year, which includes all members of the school community, board members, and parent/guardians. Free food and sports activities highlight the day's events.
- a pep assembly in the football stands the day before Homecoming to recognize all fall sports teams, coaches, and support staff. This gathering also features the mascot, school song, and distribution of small flags with the school colors to wave at the game.
- hosting the senior prom in the gym, with juniors decorating according to an appropriate theme; underclassmen supervise the "carnival" games and sports attractions at the prom lockdown the remainder of the weekend. All school clubs and all students participate.
- a talent show with several different casts and sponsors encourage all-school participation

The candidate also reveals suggestions about emphasizing the school's mission and its vision of learning for students, specifically targeting teachers' efforts at Central. The following opportunities for administrators, especially the principal, emerge:

- class visitations from the superintendent and the principal so that every teacher in every department of the school is observed "in action": a year-long emphasis

- notes that express the administration's recognition of teacher efforts and professionalism as they occur, including writing helpful mid-term reports, serving on special committees and school improvement efforts, anticipating a problem and suggesting a solution, handling a crisis, and similar efforts
- remaining teacher-accessible with special rotating office hours and visits to the teachers' lunch room, work/xerox room, and lounge (in order to receive suggestions for improvement and share concerns)
- support and encouragement of attendance at conventions, conferences and workshops, allowing presentations at faculty meetings so that effective instructional practices are spotlighted throughout the year
- starting each faculty meeting with teacher concerns related to programs, policies, rules, and problems; in addition, focusing on answers to the question "How are you responding to Central's vision of learning for students and making it a reality in your classrooms? Spread the good news with all of us!"
- creating a monthly policy committee chaired by the principal to review concerns raised by any member of the school community—policies may need changing
- hosting a faculty breakfast or steak fry at the close of the year; recognizing outstanding efforts toward the mission and vision
- monitoring the halls between classes, daily, and encouraging all administrators and counselors to do so
- recognizing teacher efforts via monthly *Notes from the Principal's Desk* newsletter, as well as at board meetings
- scheduling board meeting presentations featuring teacher and student successes; highlighting a different subject area and special units studied, contests and competitions entered, test scores, etc.

Discussion Questions

1 If a principal devotes as much attention to encouraging schoolwide attention to the school's mission and to the vision of learning for students as this candidate suggests, how can the administrator get

any "real" work done? Will a principal run the risk of neglecting other important aspects of school business?

2 What prevents these suggestions from being "token" approaches rather than gestures from a truly committed principal? How does one avoid "just going through the motions"?

3 Are the suggestions able to be adapted to a variety of school settings, student populations, and staff members? Might these only work in suburban high schools, for example?

4 What other measures has the principal candidate not considered, in view of a school's vision via symbols, ceremonies, and traditions? What has worked well in schools that you know of?

5 Does a principal need to appoint a committee to conduct a needs assessment rather than plan activities the principal feels are important? Describe the ideal blend of administrative and professional staff involvement in guiding the efforts of everyone in the building toward realizing the school's vision of learning for all students.

Comments

A principal helps to "set the tone" of a building. A sense of pride in a school's traditions and uniquenesses and the ownership one feels in the school are learned and shared. A good building climate, characterized by students' involvement in academics, one staffed by teachers who love their jobs and are enthusiastic about and committed to the school's mission and to the vision of learning for students, affects everyone involved in education. A principal must center efforts on providing for the academic and social growth of all students; teachers need to become fully engaged in the process. Full commitment to the school's mission and its vision of learning for students requires a series of strategies all year long.

PERFORMANCE OBJECTIVE

THE ADMINISTRATOR FACILITATES
PROCESSES AND ENGAGES IN
ACTIVITIES ENSURING THAT
—The core beliefs of the school vision are
  modeled for all stakeholders.

Case Study 4

Sample Mission Statement of District 203

District 203 is a student-centered community whose members strive to challenge all students to the best of their abilities so that they become independent wage earners, lifelong learners, and good citizens. A range of choices is available in academics and extracurricular activities to facilitate student growth. All who work in the district are committed to students, their development, self-actualization, and self-confidence.

Reaction

Almost 35% of District 203 employees have been teaching in the district for 15–20 years, and some have verbalized their puzzlement about the recently revised mission of the district and the new vision of learning. They protest that these are just educationese, buzz words. The German teacher, a spokesperson for many like-minded individuals, visits the principal: "We have been challenging students for nearly 20 years," she begins. "You don't need to tell us to do things differently. Students have many choices on this campus. They are very lucky." Their conversation continues for nearly 30 minutes (actually, the administrator listens), and the principal realizes this group is not in favor of change or the new vision for the district.

Discussion Questions

1 How can the principal elicit the support and cooperation of all district teachers, in view of the new emphasis on students?

2 What steps can the district take to get students and teachers excited about academic challenges?

3 Explain how district faculty and staff can be encouraged to model the basic beliefs in the mission statement.

Comments

In order to elicit the cooperation and support of all faculty and staff, administrators have to focus attention on the new direction and efforts thereof. One committed superintendent, for example, initiated a Challenge Curriculum so that student transcripts might reflect their academic achievement beyond the basic requirements. That district also started a prestigious Academic Bowl Game and created a link to local colleges so that students could attend and get credit for advanced classes. The superintendent also worked with a new schedule that allowed students to elect enrichment offerings and supervised independent study courses during the summer and most mornings, the latter from 6:45 to 8:00 A.M. Publicity about these efforts drew attention to the new focus, along with ongoing dialogues with teachers during faculty and board meetings (demonstrations and explanations). Adding new extracurricular offerings will also help: the first issue of a creative writing magazine was scheduled to appear in the spring. These examples help to create interest and involvement of students and staff.

PERFORMANCE OBJECTIVE

THE ADMINISTRATOR FACILITATES
PROCESSES AND ENGAGES IN
ACTIVITIES ENSURING THAT
—The vision is developed with and among
stakeholders.

Case Study 5

District 203 has a rough draft of its new mission statement. However, there is concern among administrators about eliciting input and consensus, if not support, among stakeholders in the district. The principal reviews available alternatives:

- Use one issue of the district newsletter to explain the vision and mission, as well as the new standards mandated by the state office of education.

- Give the local newspaper's education reporter a fact sheet about changes in the district; invite the reporter to write a series of features about the topic and other new trends in education.
- Distribute surveys. Student opinion can be obtained from a written survey with check-off and open-ended questions (to be completed during an extended home room period). Also, a separate survey might be mailed to all parent/guardians.
- Speak to Rotary and Kiwanis organizations at their regular meetings, explaining the new focus.
- Devote one board meeting to discussion of the rough draft. Publicize extensively and accept all input. Ask a committee to report back in one month with a final draft.
- Contact the 25 parent/guardians who attended the first open meeting on the mission and vision topic. Ask each one to contact 10 community people and have those contacted read the rough draft and submit changes or offer suggestions (evolve a form for this), but also have an open phone line between 1 and 2:00 P.M. daily for the next four weeks to take calls and comments.

Discussion Questions

1 Has the principal considered all viable options? What other steps should be taken to gather input?
2 What is the best approach to involve faculty and staff members?
3 Parent/guardians are very busy—how can one ensure that surveys are returned and/or opinions verbalized?
4 How about contacting former administrators and teachers, members of the League of Women Voters, university professors, librarians, and others you feel are necessary?

Comments

Issues related to changes in education, such as a new vision of learning and a mission statement, must be discussed from a knowledge base. Only then can involvement in the topics occur. Enthusiasm follows when stakeholders know they are contributing to an important dialogue and making a difference in the education of young people. However, input must be solicited and valued. All of us are used to participating in committees, meeting long and working hard—only to see our roles were "simply advisory." We must make clear to those involved in such discussions that their input is vital. Tell everyone what their involvement means and what they will get out of participating.

PERFORMANCE OBJECTIVE

THE ADMINISTRATOR FACILITATES
PROCESSES AND ENGAGES IN
ACTIVITIES ENSURING THAT
—The contributions of school community
members to the realization of the vision are
recognized and celebrated.

Case Study 6

Shorewood School had seen some difficult times in the past decade. Neighborhood and community changes put the school clientele at risk. Attendance was declining, while crime and gang participation were rising. Mrs. Smith, the principal, had seen Shorewood through the good times and now faced a variety of negative influences. She was a fighter, however, determined not to accept the demise of Shorewood.

Mrs. Smith began to call parents, explaining the effects of changes on the school. She also contacted the media who came to the school and did informational segments, both for the newspaper and the evening news. Much to Mrs. Smith's surprise, a group of parents came to her and said that they were concerned about the problems and offered to help. Their efforts included tutoring programs to help students who were in danger of failing, support groups to talk with students about the importance of completing school, volunteer services such as day care for teenage mothers, transportation for those students who might not otherwise attend classes, and on-site security monitoring so that undesirable persons were not able to interfere with the learning processes.

Slowly, attendance rates began to rise, and Shorewood experienced an upward climb. Mrs. Smith knew that she could not have accomplished what had transpired without the help of all the parent volunteers as well as those teachers who refused to give in and give up.

Mrs. Smith arranged with the cafeteria staff to host a dinner at the school to thank the people who had contributed to help the needy students of Shorewood. She distributed certificates of recognition to the volunteers. She also saw to it that the media was in attendance to ensure additional recognition.

Discussion Questions

1 How would you have handled the situation of declining attendance and gang participation at Shorewood?
2 What would have happened if the parents had refused to become involved in the volunteer process?
3 What other low-cost/no-cost measures could Mrs. Smith have used to recognize the contributions of the teachers and the volunteers?
4 How important is it to involve the superintendent in a project like this?
5 How important is it to involve the media in a project like this?
6 Could media involvement have backfired on Mrs. Smith and what was happening at Shorewood?

PERFORMANCE OBJECTIVE

THE ADMINISTRATOR FACILITATES
PROCESSES AND ENGAGES IN
ACTIVITIES ENSURING THAT
—Progress toward the vision and mission is
communicated to all stakeholders.

Case Study 7

Mission Statement

District 203 is a student-centered community whose members strive to challenge all students to the best of their abilities so that they become independent wage earners, lifelong learners, and good citizens. A range of choices is available in academics and extracurricular activities to facilitate student growth. All who work in the district are committed to students, their development, self-actualization, and self-confidence.

A Vision of Learning

District 203 encourages independent student learners who assume an increasing share of responsibility for their own learning. Students exhibit the use of analytical frameworks and creative problem-solving. They test conclusions and report results; they reveal an interest in learning beyond course requirements.

At the monthly administrative team meeting, participants brainstorm about "spotlighting" schoolwide progress toward the school's mission and vision of learning for students enrolled in District 203.

Some ideas emerge, including

- quarterly faculty "progress reports" per department revealing noteworthy student efforts in all academic courses and in nonacademic involvements, specifically geared to the mission and vision statements
- special presentations for the board of education
- a showcase of independent study student projects, a spring "Academic Fair"
- compiling or quantifying the contents of student portfolios per grade level, allowing students to explain their efforts to small groups of peers as well as inviting participation of local junior high students
- inviting local media and student newspaper representatives to see the student portfolios and pick up a detailed fact sheet that explains their content
- spring Open House for parent/guardians and community members with displays of student work
- student presentations for service clubs and organizations throughout the community

Discussion Questions

1 How can administrators encourage teachers and students to work toward the ideals of the mission and vision statements, but discourage students from "busy work" or projects that look great but have little real substance or value?

2 What other methods might administrators utilize to include community people and businesses in the district efforts toward realizing the mission and vision of learning? For example, might a local business offer samples of its budget and explain accounting practices to select mathematics classes? Might other business representatives discuss sales and service projections and plans for promotional efforts in terms of targeting larger groups of potential customers?

3 A local theater group presents four plays a year. They seek help in all aspects of staging their presentations. How might the group benefit from student help, and how might students learn from the experience?

4 The local television station is very open to input from the school district. Is it unrealistic to expect them to interview faculty and staff and students, to host a show on student efforts toward the vision of learning and toward "new directions" for district schools? How can the station benefit?

5 Describe your district's successful strategies to call attention to the vision of learning and communicating students' progress thereof.

Comments

A district's full commitment to all aspects of students' growth, development, and learning is a tall order. Because full curricula and specific goals and objectives dictate daily lessons, administrators need to articulate the importance of the vision of learning. They also must explain how progress emerges from careful analysis of course content. In addition, specific suggestions and models are necessary. Teachers might use inservice days at the outset of each school year to discuss and plan for tailoring lessons to the mission and vision. They might visit other districts and research notable student efforts countrywide. Progress meetings throughout the year might facilitate continued efforts toward meeting school goals. Every teacher will have to "buy into" the vision and remain committed to its ideals; each teacher must see colleagues actively involved in rethinking coursework and planning new learning packets. Teachers must also realize the administrators' priority lies in sometimes changing the delivery of instruction, as well as assessments and evaluations that follow.

PERFORMANCE OBJECTIVE
THE ADMINISTRATOR FACILITATES
PROCESSES AND ENGAGES IN
ACTIVITIES ENSURING THAT
—The school community is involved in school
  improvement efforts.

Case Study 8

Principal John Evans opened up the monthly faculty meeting by saying, "The state has sent us these new requirements for school improvement. You know how they come up with something new about every year or so. I noticed that one requirement this year is to involve people from the community in the formulation of our goals and implementation of these goals for improving the school. I wanted to invite some of you who have taught here for awhile to get your opinion on how to do this."

Rex Pearson, a science teacher, said, "I don't understand why we should have parents or other community people involved in this project. They are well-meaning people, but they do not know what we are doing now. You just have to spend so much time explaining what we are doing. We could have the whole thing done if we would just do it ourselves."

Joan Peters, from the English department, replied, "But, Rex, that is the point. The people in this town should know what is going on in their schools. We should take the time to tell them and get their ideas. So, it takes an extra session. So what?"

Discussion Questions

1 Do you agree with either Rex or Joan? Why?

2 Is it really important for community people who are not parents to understand what goes on in the schools? If so, whose responsibility is it to keep them informed? And, how do you do it?

3 Assuming that principal Evans has to involve community members, regardless of anyone's opinion, how should he choose these people? Or, is he even the person who should choose them?

4 Are there certain qualifications or qualities you would suggest for the people to be selected from the community? Why did you pick these?

5 Once the people are selected, how would you communicate with them initially? Through the mail, by phone, or with a meeting, or some combination?

6 Assuming you are the principal or chair of the first meeting of the group (community people and teachers), make up an agenda for that first meeting. Why did you put these items on the list and in that order?

7 How would you determine when and where to hold the meeting? What do you do about people who cannot come or do not show up?

8 Are there any special physical arrangements you would suggest for the meeting to be successful or is that important?

PERFORMANCE OBJECTIVE

THE ADMINISTRATOR FACILITATES
PROCESSES AND ENGAGES IN
ACTIVITIES ENSURING THAT
—The school community is involved in school
  improvements efforts.

Case Study 9

A seasoned, experienced principal, this school leader feels lucky that the board members took the lead and developed a tentative mission statement and a first-draft vision of learning paragraph for the district. The principal knows district personnel well; aware of the factions that include the Old Guard, the Young Turks, the coaches and PE people, and the snooty subject specialists, she realizes their achieving consensus on any issue is improbable, if not a dream.

Also, community involvement in the school has never been the norm; your only input is protests about higher property taxes and, heaven forbid, plans to expand, rebuild or remodel the building or take care of grounds. Parent/guardians? It is unusual to get more than 25 of them at any event. A handful of mature young people, including the newspaper editor, can be relied upon, however.

Consideration of these facts motivates the principal's own involvement in rewriting and editing the mission and vision documents. She plans to spearhead the implementation of the content of both documents, viewing her role as the key to the success of any changes in the district. What other choices does she have?

Discussion Questions

1 How does a school leader involve school faculty and staff, parent/guardians, and community members in the substantial work of fine-tuning the vision of learning and its implementation in the district?

2 When, in reality, only the school administrators and maybe select dedicated "snooty subject specialists" are interested in reform efforts related to district improvement, is it not clear that an administrator should proceed, along with like-minded individuals?

3 Community members in this district, including some parents who champion special interest issues, are notoriously suspicious about any changes in local educational efforts. What efforts might school leaders make to create awareness of, if not encourage support of and participation in, these important changes for students?

Comments

Involvement in improving educational efforts for district students yields important results. Divergent opinions must be heard; they can help group members create more universal views of things. Agreed-upon compromises can result. At times, allowing young people to become involved in recruiting their parents and community people may be an option. Appeals to people's basic willingness to lend a hand and their desire to improve local educational efforts are starting points. What techniques can school leaders use to encourage participation in the substantial efforts and time commitments involved? How can administrators target the end-result—in short, what's in it for those who expend the time and effort necessary?

PERFORMANCE OBJECTIVE

THE ADMINISTRATOR FACILITATES
PROCESSES AND ENGAGES IN
ACTIVITIES ENSURING THAT
—The school community is involved in school
  improvement efforts.

Case Study 10

The principal of this suburban high school recognizes challenges when he sees them. "When it rains, it pours," he complains at the administrative team meeting. "What can we do about these issues related to school improvement efforts?" He reviews a list of items needing attention.

- The halls are littered with paper, and the maintenance staff is already overwhelmed. Also, graffiti is beginning to appear in the bathrooms, on lockers, and on desks.

- Many students are ignoring the heavy-duty garbage cans in the cafeteria, throwing waste paper and food on the floor, or just leaving trays with food and non-food items for someone else to pick up. The teachers assigned as cafeteria monitors cannot supervise every single table!

- School spirit, if not class spirit, seems at a low ebb. "There's so little involvement that not enough students have expressed interest in Homecoming activities or building floats. I can understand their dislike of selling candy bars and other fund-raisers, but Homecoming has been a big thing in this district."

- Teachers and administrators face the overwhelming responsibility, in view of new reform efforts and state mandates, to review all courses offered and the objectives that govern them.

- Sports attendance is flagging. Only a few parents attended the pre-season swim meet or the wrestling team's inter-squad meet last week. Student involvement is nonexistent. What should be done to involve students at all grade levels so that they utilize their talents?

Discussion Questions

1 Are some years "off" times for participation in school activities? May students yield to pressures to be "cool" and uninvolved?

2 How can a principal encourage participation and build school and grade-level spirit if no one is interested? Should that be part of the job responsibility? Should the responsibility for involvement be written into the goals and objectives governing students' participation in school? Is involvement really important, anyway?

3 Students learn that they have responsibilities to others in school settings. What ideas seem workable in view of littered hallways and a messy cafeteria? These areas cannot be overlooked too long.

4 How can teachers help to encourage students to get involved, if they, themselves, tire of their responsibilities? The faculty is a good one, heavily involved in teaching and extracurricular activities as it is.

Comments

Administrators cannot mandate school spirit and involvement, but how can they encourage both? Students can gain so much more than academic credits from extracurricular sports and activities. Why does participation wane some years? Also, faculty and staff face quite a commitment in reviewing all the course goals and objectives; it will take almost the entire year for this project alone. How can administrators involve everyone—students, faculty, and staff—in the school, its offerings, and in their responsibilities?

PERFORMANCE OBJECTIVE

THE ADMINISTRATOR FACILITATES
PROCESSES AND ENGAGES IN
ACTIVITIES ENSURING THAT
—The vision shapes the educational
  programs, plans, and actions.
—An implementation plan is developed in
  which objectives and strategies to achieve
  the vision and goals are clearly articulated.
—The vision, mission, and implementation
  plans are regularly monitored, evaluated,
  and revised.

Case Study 11

Mission Statement

District 203 is a student-centered community whose members strive to challenge all students to the best of their abilities so that they become independent wage earners, lifelong learners, and good citizens. A range of choices is available in academics and extracurricular activities to facilitate student growth. All who work in the district are committed to students, their development, self-actualization, and self-confidence.

A Vision of Learning

District 203 encourages independent student learners who assume an increasing share of responsibility for their own learning. Students exhibit the use of analytical frameworks and creative problem-solving. They test conclusions and report results; they reveal an interest in learning beyond course requirements.

Several proposals have emerged for keeping the mission alive:

1 A committee must review all programs and courses offered in the district, specifically looking for connections to the mission statement and vision; suggestions for changes in course content will be made, if there seems to be insufficient emphasis on the mission and vision. This needs assessment may give direction to changes that must originate in each department of the school.

2 A separate committee must review extracurricular offerings, again with the mission statement and vision in mind—with power to recommend addition of new supplemental activities or clubs as needed. This is also a needs assessment.

3 An oversight committee will "evaluate" adherence to the mission and vision; department chairs, for example, will specify how all department teachers have altered teaching style or content in terms of the new focus (challenging students; student focus).

4 A consultant will be hired to listen to the "evaluations" of the oversight committee and to offer suggestions about how to meet the specifics of the mission and vision. School administrators will have input into the final decisions.

5 A research committee will visit other schools that are implementing changes aligned to the mission and vision of their districts; committee members will also review salient literature on this subject.

Discussion Questions

1 The review of all school programs and offerings, as well as extracurricular activities, is so complex and so time-consuming as to be almost impossible to carry out. How else could the review be conducted? Should two committees be given this much power?

2 Bringing in an outside consultant is questionable: This person is not in the district and does not understand its philosophy or this new orientation. Wouldn't it be better to have board members oversee the efforts?

3 Considerable school time may be wasted by a research committee visiting other districts; how can these visitations be conducted so that District 203 benefits? Isn't it just as valuable to have personnel and administrators from other districts come to District 203 faculty meetings and explain their successes?

4 Teachers are already stressed to their limits with preparation for classes and extra-duty assignments. There is no way they will agree to serve on additional committees—or is there?

5 What kind of a time frame are we talking about here? These meetings might take up so much time and become so bogged down in debate that nothing is accomplished. How can the committee efforts be maximized for greatest success?

6 What provisions for monitoring, evaluating, and revising needed changes should be established, in terms of immediate and long-range efforts? Checkpoints and follow-up activities are necessary.

Comments

Review the dynamics of successful committee work. Think of teachers' groups that accomplish a given task or respond to substantial projects like instituting new reforms and/or getting ready for accreditation visits. What suggestions can you give the faculty and staff of District 203 as they think about and plan for making the vision of learning and the school's mission a reality in all areas of learning?

THE ADMINISTRATOR FACILITATES
PROCESSES AND ENGAGES IN
ACTIVITIES ENSURING THAT
—Assessment data related to student
  learning are used to develop the school
  vision and goals.

Case Study 12

In a rare display of solidarity, the English and social studies department chairpersons arrange a special 90-minute session with the principal. "George, we've got a problem here," begins the English chair.

Both department heads share their concerns: Students entering the high school cannot write unified, coherent single paragraphs; spelling, grammar/usage, and punctuation errors interfere with their attempts to convey ideas on examinations; and verbal communication skills reveal that even students in honors sections of English and social studies fail in their efforts to problem solve and take part in effective discussions that move toward resolution of issues. By year's end, ninth graders' scores on the SST (State Standards Test) confirm these impressions.

The principal and the chairpersons create several new goals:

- Ninth graders must pass (85% mastery) a rigorous grammar/usage, punctuation, and spelling test before they enroll in tenth grade English and social studies classes.
- Ninth graders will show that they are able to lead or participate in discussions of sample unit-related problems.
- At year's end, ninth graders must demonstrate appropriate rhetorical strategies in an "Exit Essay Exam," including a sense of organization and full development of ideas, writing to a specific audience, and concluding via a restatement of pertinent points or summarizing topic sentence or thesis. Given only a topic (i.e., concern for the environment or the importance of a single historical event), each student must write a fully developed and original paragraph in an hour's time.

The three also agree that the school's vision of learning must include these new imperatives, and they draft a sample statement:

A Communication-Based Vision of Learning

Effective communication skills facilitate students' plans for continuing their education or pursuing a variety of job and career goals upon graduation. Our students are confident, able discussion leaders and effective group participants. They understand and apply strategies to create interesting, insightful, and developed prose essays (short and long essays), and they write clear, correct, error-free responses to a variety of rhetorical types, such as argument, explanation, definition, etc.

Discussion Questions

1 Are the department chairpersons and principal overreacting in creating a new communication skills emphasis for students? Are the new requirements at year's end, in addition to the SST, unrealistic?

2 What provisions can be made for students who do not acquire 85% mastery? Summer school? Individual tutorials? The three may have overlooked this problem.

3 Are communication skills more important than mathematical reasoning and understanding scientific methods and concepts? How can they create changes without input from the entire faculty? Advise them about steps to take in order to gain compliance with their new vision for students, if you feel their attention to communication skills is indicated.

4 If students do not exhibit appropriate communication skill levels, should remediation programs related to the causes of their problems be investigated first? Some may have learning problems, for whom these new communication skills are beyond their mastery. What to do in those cases?

5 What kinds of assessment data are most reliable in revealing student strengths and weaknesses?

6 Comment on the commitment of your school or district to teaching students excellent communication skills. What works well? Describe assessment strategies used.

Comments

Communication skills, verbal and written, impact students' success once they graduate. The ability to present ideas is particularly critical in an information age. Practical applications, such as on-the-job reports, presenting one's qualifications at a job interview, and discussing the merchandising of a company's new product, may be necessary to supplement teachers' instructional efforts. Employers routinely expect schools to teach skills and students to exhibit mastery levels; parent/guardians and community members want students to be able to succeed in the workplace. We may have to support renewed and vigorous efforts aimed at increasing students' skill levels in all subject areas, *including* more vigorous math and science-related learning. All are critical. How to do so may be subject to intense discussion and debate, but the dialogue must begin. Students' futures are at stake.

PERFORMANCE OBJECTIVE

THE ADMINISTRATOR FACILITATES
PROCESSES AND ENGAGES IN
ACTIVITIES ENSURING THAT
—Assessment data related to student
learning are used to develop the school
vision and goals.

Case Study 13

"I am glad you could all attend the meeting this evening," said Mrs. Alvarez, as she glanced around the auditorium and noticed most of those in attendance were seated in the back. "This is just like church. Why don't you come down to the front, so I will not have to use a microphone."

"Thank you for relocating. As you know, our test scores are back. I know that getting ready for this assessment test has been both difficult and time-consuming. I am not going to try to minimize the impact of these tests. We are definitely under a microscope. It is my belief that we need to examine the test as a whole, and then evaluate student performance. I want to say from the outset that I am not blaming or accusing anyone on this faculty. I want this test to be considered as a learning tool. Assessment tests are with us; I do not see them disappearing into the sunset.''

John Pierce, a new teacher, seemed visibly upset when he raised his hand, glanced around at his colleagues, and asked, "What can we do to help our students?"

Mrs. Alvarez nodded as she answered, "That is just what I am talking about, John. We need to look at the scores and then we need to examine our curricular offerings as they relate to our school goals and our vision of learning. If our programs need revision or alteration in any way, we must move, and move quickly, to address those needs. I said we were under a microscope. I think the media and the parents will question the scores. I am quite frank when I say that the scores are truly disappointing. I know you are all good teachers, but I am genuinely concerned about the curricular content. We must be proactive. I truly believe that if we mount an offensive to look at current offerings as they relate to the tests, to students' needs, and to our goals and vision, we will, at least partially, exonerate ourselves and help our students at the same time. Do you all agree with my assessment?"

Discussion Questions

1 How important are student assessments to you as an administrator?
2 What would you have done if you were chairing the meeting that Mrs. Alvarez held?
3 Should the faculty fear assessment instruments, or should they embrace them as tools for measurement and change?
4 How would you react to media and parental criticism, and how would you handle it?
5 Would you have blamed your staff for low test scores; if so, why?
6 Do you agree with Mrs. Alvarez' approach to the assessment problem?
7 Now that the faculty has the scores and knows they are poor, how can they use this information to change the curriculum? to assess the goals and vision of the school?

PERFORMANCE OBJECTIVE

THE ADMINISTRATOR FACILITATES
PROCESSES AND ENGAGES IN
ACTIVITIES ENSURING THAT
—Relevant demographic data pertaining to
   students and their families are used in
   developing the school mission and goals.

Case Study 14

Ron McGee, principal of Palmer High School, was meeting with his administrative staff. "We are in an unusual situation. We are all new to the district and to our positions. I feel very much like the dog who used to chase cars and finally caught one! We need to be certain that we are meeting the wants and needs of our community and our students." As he looked around the table at his administrative team, he noticed a couple of his assistant principals glancing at each other. "I really need your input on this matter," he said.

Mrs. Warner said tentatively, "We need to be certain that our offerings are relevant to the students."

At that point, Mr. Caldwell chimed in, "We need to be offering courses that truly teach life skills. We do not need advanced calculus, nor do we need a course in quantum physics."

"What do you suggest?" asked their principal.

Mrs. Warner, who had curricular responsibilities, answered, "John is right. Life skills are very important. We need to look at our population. These are disadvantaged students from an impoverished setting. For instance, our counseling staff tells us that have an abundance of teen pregnancies. I suggest we offer some courses related to health and parenting skills. We also need courses relevant to the lifestyle of our students and their families. The police records and our data from child protective services tell us that we are dealing with students with drug and gang involvement. We must institute courses that address these concerns."

"I think," said Mr. McGee, "that we may be on the right track. I want to run some ideas by the superintendent. Not only do our courses need to reflect the demographics, but our mission and goals also must relate to our unique student populace, their growth and progress."

Discussion Questions

1 How does a principal decide to what extent the curriculum is driven by the demographics of the district?

2 How much involvement should there be between outside social agencies and the school?

3 Were Mr. McGee and his administrative staff correct in monitoring and using assessment of relevant demographics to revamp course offerings?

4 Why did Mr. McGee involve his entire administrative staff?

5 Why did Mr. McGee want to involve the superintendent in what had been discussed?

PERFORMANCE OBJECTIVE

THE ADMINISTRATOR FACILITATES
PROCESSES AND ENGAGES IN
ACTIVITIES ENSURING THAT
—Relevant demographic data pertaining to
   students and their families are used in
   developing the school mission and goals.

Case Study 15

"New Data Show How We're Changing" reads the headline. A front-page local news feature describes the results of socioeconomic studies of the areas surrounding the high school. An administrative team meeting occurs that morning, and participants review the feature story and some of the data provided.

The population consists of the following demographics:

- Residents aged 60 and older represent 55% of the population.
- Recent move-ins and "transient" families account for 30% of the resident population, with school-age children present in 22% of these units.
- A 15% "stable" population, residents of 10+ years, include people aged 20–55 years.

The job index shows a roughly 10% decline in availability of spending power; job surveys indicate that a stability is projected overall for the next 10 years, despite the 5% job loss figure.

Administrators review changes in the school they are aware of currently:

- increases in students' eligibility for free and reduced-price lunches
- increases in discipline and academic problems—students acting out, unprepared for classes, problems with attention, increased need for tutorial or remedial instruction
- decline in parent/guardian participation (PTA, Open House, conferences, disciplinary hearings)

In order to realize part of the mission of the school district, some changes must occur. The statement that the school leaders cite reveals that "Center High School graduates are prepared for additional academic study as well as entry in a variety of job and career areas. Their basic skills profile is above average overall, especially in communication skills, mathematics, science, and technological awareness."

Administrators discuss some options:

- exploring technical and vocational alternatives available through community colleges for students, including programs for high school students showing special interest and aptitude
- determining why parent/guardian participation in their children's education has declined (make increased participation a goal)
- creating conference and Open House alternative days and nights, even the school providing transportation for parent/guardian meetings
- seeking psychologists' input on discipline, attendance, counseling alternatives
- spearheading campaign to create a community adolescent center (psychological services, motivational efforts, tutorials)
- creating "New Options" curriculum based on students' informed goal setting for postgraduation
- utilizing community support services more fully, drawing in senior citizen community members

- beginning tutorial and remedial programs to meet needs revealed in student tests and state/national test scores
- investigating ESL opportunities and programs

Discussion Questions

1 What guidelines must administrators follow in reviewing sociological surveys of their communities? What sources and specifics are particularly useful in planning school-related programs and services?

2 Is it possible for administrators to draw up various "Preparedness Plan" agendas in advance of community changes? Or can a school community stand firm and maintain its existing level of programs and services, its mission and goals, *making students and parents adapt?*

3 How can administrators prepare students, teachers, and the school staff for potential challenges in the school setting? To what extent must every member of the school community, parent/guardians, and the community at large be apprised of changes? Can the path toward these changes be smoothed out?

4 What changes is your district experiencing, if any? What changes have you observed or know about in other districts? How have changes been addressed? What successes and lapses can you describe in view of the experiences of these districts and schools?

5 How does an administrator work to achieve consensus and compliance among teachers and members of the professional staff in their responses to the school's mission and goals? What problems (and solutions) can you foresee? How can administrators set high expectations and monitor progress toward realizing the mission and goals of the school?

Comments

Change is inevitable, even for individual schools with long-standing traditions and some degree of stability. Though their role may not be easy, administrators are agents and monitors of change. Moving students toward social responsibility and growth, creating educational programs and services that they need, now and in the future, are our primary responsibilities. It is up to district administrators to seek ongoing input about changes that impact students' lives, locally, regionally, and globally. To do any less may be to underestimate our ability to prepare students for their world tomorrow.

PERFORMANCE OBJECTIVES

THE ADMINISTRATOR FACILITATES
PROCESSES AND ENGAGES IN
ACTIVITIES ENSURING THAT
—Barriers to achieving the vision are
   identified, clarified, and addressed.

Case Study 16

The faculty members were discussing the documents they were writing for an accreditation visit by a regional agency. John said, "We need to state that our goal is to train students for the world of work. If they cannot get jobs after they leave here, we have not done our job."

Mary, another high school teacher, said, "Sure, work is important, but our purpose is not to train workers. We are here to educate young people—to train their minds, if we are to train anything."

Tom, a veteran teacher, replied, "I sorta agree with Mary, but I think we train students' minds for a particular thing: higher education. I know that not all of our students go to four-year universities, but almost all of them go to some kind of higher education. Even the few who go into the military have to go to school!"

Discussion Questions

1 Sometimes it is difficult to agree on a school's purpose. If you were the principal in attendance at this discussion, how could you take this important discussion and use it to help identify the school's purpose?

2 Are the above opinions somewhat typical, or are they exaggerated in the case study?

3 Why do teachers in the same school have such divergent opinions about the purpose of the school? Is this beneficial or harmful?

4 Besides teacher opinions, what other barriers to establishing a common purpose can you think of which may need to be addressed? How would you address each one of these?

5 Is it important at all to even have a written vision or purpose or to take time to discuss it? Or, is it useful only to complete reports like the one in the case study or in required state reports?

PERFORMANCE OBJECTIVE

THE ADMINISTRATOR FACILITATES
PROCESSES AND ENGAGES IN
ACTIVITIES ENSURING THAT
—Barriers to achieving the vision are
  identified, clarified, and addressed.

Case Study 17

The superintendent, board of education members, and administrators at the high school have been approached with questions, concerns, and complaints from students, parent/guardians, and community members. The reactions reflect changes in the district, including altered course requirements indicative of new and more rigorous expectations; required parent/guardian attendance at various conferences, back-to-school nights, and "Introduction to the New Year" programs; a revised student Code of Conduct; and increased security staff personnel in the building.

As one parent asked, "What's going on at the school?" Even some board members are becoming nervous due to the questions they are asked.

"Let's define where we are and where we expect students to be," challenges the principal. "We need to give confident responses to questions and complaints."

The meeting identifies the causes of changes in the school—perceived "barriers" to students achieving the ideals of the vision of learning statement. These include

- course content revision in order that students achieve specific objectives and skill mastery (content did not always dovetail objectives)
- course content requiring continuous updating to reflect technological changes but also a changed global economy; more to be expected of tomorrow's workforce
- parental/guardian involvement in students' efforts: Administrators perceive the need for marshalling every source available to encourage and reinforce student success. Parents are expected to monitor homework efforts and students' free hours.
- students influenced by peers and the media moved toward realization that society holds them accountable for appropriate behavior and that there are consequences for infringement of rules: Behavioral standards start in school settings; regular, daily attendance is vital, as is students' acceptance of their responsibility for their behavior and academic records
- security personnel monitoring "hot" areas of the building and overseeing places that cannot be otherwise secured: The guarantee for a safe, secure, orderly environment comes at the price of additional support personnel.
- counselors' intervention—perceived as necessary to reach every student with data supporting students' strengths and weaknesses: Educational and career options are targeted in a renewed, ongoing effort.

Discussion Questions

1 What steps can school administrators take to reach all members of the school community and the community at large to explain changes like those described above? Is it necessary to hire a public relations specialist? Should explanations precede changes?

2 What should be the role of the board of education in facilitating school changes to meet the vision of learning for all students?

3 Give the administrators advice about how to manage and monitor far-reaching school changes. Can well-meaning boards and school leaders legislate too many changes too quickly?

4 Discuss changes like those described above that have occurred in your building or in other schools you know about. Describe successes (and success strategies), as well as "near-misses." What caused the "near-misses"?

Comments

Commitment to a vision of learning for students requires superb planning and management skills. School leaders might well engage every member of the school community and the community at large in their efforts. Invariably, barriers or roadblocks will surface; these can be identified, studied, and addressed. Prevailing attitudes, expectations for levels of achievement, degree of comfort with change, and acceptance of new and/or increasing budgetary expenses vary. An overriding consideration for all students' academic success and social growth may be a way of addressing questions and complaints. Most people are interested in how changes will create increased educational opportunities for students and ensure their chances for postgraduation success.

PERFORMANCE OBJECTIVES

THE ADMINISTRATOR FACILITATES
PROCESSES AND ENGAGES IN
ACTIVITIES ENSURING THAT
—Needed resources are sought and obtained
  to support the implementation of the school
  mission and goals.

Case Study 18

The principal, Dr. Arlene Gregory, was concerned that students were not receiving appropriate curricular offerings at Filmore Junior/Senior High School. In a recent walk-through of her building, she spent time with members of the business department faculty, who assailed her with horror stories of outdated equipment. Mr. Donahue, the department chair, stated that it was tough enough to train tomorrow's workforce with today's equipment, but it was virtually impossible to train tomorrow's workforce with yesterday's equipment. When Dr. Gregory questioned Mr. Donahue's meaning, she was told that Filmore had very few word processors and that many of the students were still forced to learn typing skills on outdated typewriters. "We cannot afford to send students into the modern workplace with such antiquated skills," said Mr. Donahue. Several of the teachers nodded their heads in agreement.

"I heartily agree with you, Mr. Donahue," said Dr. Gregory, as she surveyed the typing labs. "Why do we still have all of these old beat-up typewriters in service? Why haven't you requisitioned new word processors for your business labs?"

"I realize you have not been at Filmore very long, Dr. Gregory. Otherwise you would know that the business department is not a major concern in the budgetary process. We have been level funded for longer than I care to remember. We used to have a good reputation, but businesses and business leaders are beginning to get sick and tired of students graduating from here who have only read or heard about modern business practices."

"What have you done about it, Mr. Donahue?" asked Dr. Gregory.

"I have complained to your predecessor before he became superintendent, and I have complained to the school board. Unfortunately, I have met with little success."

"Since your target audience is business, I think that maybe we need to take our case to the business community. I suggest we develop an advisory board of business leaders so that they can tell us their expectations. After that, I propose that we have a breakfast here at Filmore. We can invite members of the school board as well as business leaders. It might not be a bad idea to invite some of our local legislators too. Perhaps we can get some of these people to donate equipment or additional funding. But, I assure you that if the business curriculum is an important component of Filmore's course offerings, we will do everything we can to obtain modern equipment and the necessary funding to educate well-trained students."

Discussion Questions

1 Was Dr. Gregory wise in seeking input from the various departments within her high school?

2 What level of trust did you perceive between her and Mr. Donahue?

3 Do you feel that her direct approach to the business community was inappropriate, or do you believe that it was justified?

4 Why do you think that Dr. Gregory wanted to include members of the school board in her breakfast gathering?

5 Why do you think that Dr. Gregory wanted to include members of the legislature?

6 Do you think it was appropriate for the principal and members of the department to expose the shortcomings of the business department to public scrutiny?

PERFORMANCE OBJECTIVE

THE ADMINISTRATOR FACILITATES
PROCESSES AND ENGAGES IN
ACTIVITIES ENSURING THAT
—Needed resources are sought and obtained
   to support the implementation of the school
   mission and goals.

Case Study 19

A review of the mission statement reveals the district focus:
District 203 is a student-centered community whose members strive to challenge all students to the best of their abilities so that they become independent wage earners, lifelong learners, and good citizens.

Discussion Questions

1 What learning opportunities might be included in courses that are aimed at increasing students' level of comfort with life changes, career changes, and going back to school for additional training if needed? How can students who are working at minimum-wage, part-time jobs understand the dynamics of the labor market, reengineered businesses, and the changing American economy?

2 Although many community members might argue that the skill content of academic study is more important than anything else,

is there a way to include more attention and effort to students' understanding fully their own skills, interests, talents and abilities—in terms of new career and job potentials?

3 Develop a list of local groups (i.e. Rotary, Chamber of Commerce, community government sources), who might sponsor programs directed toward students' understanding their roles as citizens of the community and the world.

4 Outline a program to increase students' understanding of and appreciation for "lifelong learning" as it may directly affect them.

Comments

Resources include people, a community's greatest asset. There are people in the school district who have a wealth of job/career and business experience and an awareness of the changes that have occurred in the world of work in the last several decades. How can we utilize better our greatest resource, our own community members—to their own benefit and to the benefit of our students? The term *resources* also includes social service agencies and trained professionals in a variety of fields and a variety of settings. Resources also include print and database materials, reference works, and the Internet. What other resources are available to schools and should be utilized, especially in view of mission statements that stress jobs, learning, and citizenship?

PERFORMANCE OBJECTIVE

THE ADMINISTRATOR FACILITATES
PROCESSES AND ENGAGES IN
ACTIVITIES ENSURING THAT
—Existing resources are used in support of
  the school vision and goals.

Case Study 20

"Mr. Knight, our superintendent, has just informed me that we need to reevaluate all of our curricular programs," said Mrs. Pena, the principal of Hamlin Middle School, as she addressed her faculty. The members of the staff gave each other meaningful glances as she said this. "I know what you are thinking. Yes, it is a lot of work, but we need to be certain that we are giving our students and our community the most we can for the tax dollars that they expend."

Mr. Torres, the social studies teacher, asked if the faculty would need to examine the school district's past position on curricular offerings. "I certainly think that would be a part of it, Mr. Torres," said Mrs. Pena. "I think we should examine the school district's mission statement as well as the mission statement that we developed three years ago when the accrediting team was in our district."

"Have things changed dramatically, Mrs. Pena, or are we just doing busy work because the superintendent believes we do not have enough to do to keep us occupied?"

"No, I do not believe that," affirmed Mrs. Pena. "I do know that the superintendent is worried about budget constraints. I also know the board has had a lot of pressure from citizens who believe we are overpaid and underworked. I honestly feel the superintendent wants to make certain that all of our existing resources are being appropriately committed and utilized. I think it is important that we 'police' ourselves to be certain that we are expending our dollars wisely, and that each of our curricular offerings reflects this."

Mrs. Goldstein, the music teacher, held up her hand to be recognized. "I just want an assurance, Mrs. Pena, that we will not lose funding. I do not think my program—and I am certain that I speak for others as well—can afford to be cut any further that it already has been."

"Thank you, Mrs. Goldstein. Let me try to reassure each of you that the purpose of this reevaluation is not to cut further, but to be certain that our resources are being used to the optimum."

Discussion Questions

1 Was the superintendent correct in ordering a reevaluation of curricular offerings?

2 Was the reaction of Mrs. Pena's staff predictable?

3 Was Mrs. Pena correct in having the staff understand the budgetary and curricular concerns of the superintendent?

4 How much impact would a mission statement have on the budget and, ultimately, the curriculum? Provide relevant examples of such impact from your own experience.

5 How would you have reacted to Mrs. Goldstein's concerns?

6 Do you feel that Mrs. Pena might be wrong in her assessment of what funding will be available?

7 If funding is cut, how will this affect her relationship with members of her staff?

8 If funding is cut, how might this affect her relationship with the superintendent?

PERFORMANCE OBJECTIVE

THE ADMINISTRATOR FACILITATES
PROCESSES AND ENGAGES IN
ACTIVITIES ENSURING THAT
—Existing resources are used in support of
the school vision and goals.

Case Study 21

"We have to look closely at our resources," J. Principal encourages administrators at the team meeting devoted to exploring a new vision of learning for students and changed goals. Principal reviews some resources.

The School Building

Principal notes that the school is in sound shape still, after 30 years' wear and tear. On-site facilities are large and can be modified to meet changing curricular requirements and experiments with various learning options. The west wing of the school is spacious and under-utilized. An ongoing maintenance and repair schedule assures administrators that the facility as a whole is an asset.

Area Technical and Vocational Center

Administrators agree that the center's offerings need publicity. Counselors need to be especially sensitive to students' aptitudes, abilities, and career interests. A committee of interested administrators will study the tech center and make more specific recommendations as they relate to the school's vision and goals.

Local Business/Industry

Principal is a member of Rotary International as well as the Chamber of Commerce. At recent meetings, he has approached the glove factory representative about a partnership with the school. He agrees to follow up the initial discussion and to contact the executive vice-president of a water and waste treatment systems company about a similar connection. Principal thinks about the possibility of their offering guest speakers from their staffs, donations of "old" computers, tutorials, internships, etc.

Community Support and Media Attention

The communities surrounding the school are proud of education's impact (school ranking and state recognitions) on real estate values. High school sports attract huge crowds, and media attention has been, on the whole, positive. Administrators may need to tap into these support networks for publicity and outreach.

The Board of Education

A stable, almost politically neutral board whose members are committed to improving all aspects of the school for students, the board has been extremely open-minded about new funding projects, pilot programs, building use and change, and new programs and curricular changes.

Teachers

An enthusiastic and vocal group of teachers has expressed interest in exploring new approaches to the delivery of instruction. They seek to research new theories about styles of learning and contact the local university's department of education. Several want to visit "light-house" schools.

The Nearby University

Principal concedes the university *could* be a good resource for the school, but he feels the dean of the College of Education is strange and distant, more a politician, and that the department chairperson "always has his nose in some obscure subject for research."

Discussion Questions

1 What are the "key" resources that most benefit schools, their mission and goals? List five of the most important. What data or specifics support these as being crucial for a district? Is an adolescent health- and related-services center within a community necessary?

2 What "local" resources might also be used to benefit the school's vision and goals for students? Use your own experience to describe these and their potential impact. Give examples to illustrate.

3 What overtures to the university representatives in the Department of Education might prove successful? How can a partnership with the university benefit the high school and vice versa?

4 Can a nearby park and lakes system/network and national forest be considered potential resources to enhance schools' efforts for students? A local mall? Downtown small businesses? Churches of many denominations? Nursing homes? Hospitals?

5 What important resources relate to technology and to the global economy? Describe their potential impact on schools' efforts.

Comments

Resources that supplement all phases of a school's educational pro-gram for students are essential additions to existing ones. The key is to connect students' needs, the programs, vision of learning for students, and school goals with appropriate resources. Determining whether key resources exist, perhaps overlooked or under-utilized, may be the priority of each department in a school. Administrators and board members can spearhead additional searches. "Where there's a will, there's a way" may apply, as students, school programs, the vision of learning, and goals determine resource needs.

PERFORMANCE OBJECTIVE

THE ADMINISTRATOR FACILITATES
PROCESSES AND ENGAGES IN
ACTIVITIES ENSURING THAT
—Existing resources are used in support of
the school vision and goals.

Case Study 22

J. Principal disagrees somewhat with the administrative team's conclusion that *outside* people and a variety of resources must be brought in to help the school address the district's vision and goals. "Why, we have a very diverse faculty and support staff right here!" he argues. "Look at all the personnel in this district—from board members down to part-time landscapers, contracted building services members, and bus drivers. We have a gold mine of people. Can't you see what I mean? Our 'program' for kids is each and every one of us!" he insists. "We don't need anyone else."

Discussion Questions

1 How might the district utilize the interest, knowledge, and experience of all faculty, staff, and contract workers to best advantage for students? Outline a proposal to tap into and utilize what these professionals can offer students. Can a list or media-style sourcebook be drawn up illustrating people's specialties? Would everyone want to participate?

2 What possibilities exist for setting up useful programs to bring together students and district personnel in non-classroom teaching

settings? Note these ideas: informal lectures and demonstrations, small group discussions based on academic departments' invitations directed toward "experts," "guest speakers," skits or dramatizations, formal presentations, dialogues with school career counselors, meetings with parent/guardians and students, and 1- or 2-week mini-courses.

3 How does a school set up a telecommunication program, monthly, with state university personnel who are experts in a variety of fields, career and job counselors, and academic advisors who describe programs available, etc.?

Comments

J. Principal has a good point: School district personnel, in many cases, know the students and their needs. They know about the data illustrating college admittance and retention rates of graduates from the district (if not, surveys of graduates at 1, 2, 3 and 5 years after graduation might be considered). Many could actually be important advisors, supplementary counselors, for students. In addition, many are aware of postsecondary vocational and technical programs available. How can they best be utilized for students? How can former graduates aid the school's efforts?

CHAPTER 4

Standard 2 Case Studies

A school administrator is an educational leader who promotes the success of all students by advocating, nurturing, and sustaining a school culture and instructional program conducive to student learning and staff professional growth.

PERFORMANCE OBJECTIVE

THE ADMINISTRATOR FACILITATES
PROCESSES AND ENGAGES IN
ACTIVITIES ENSURING THAT
—All individuals are treated with fairness,
dignity, and respect.

Case Study 23

At 4:15 on Friday afternoon, John Burns stormed into Mrs. Walker's office. He threw his books angrily onto her desk and slumped into a side chair. "I have had it," he exclaimed. Mrs. Walker, the principal, looked up and saw his anger and frustration. "What's wrong, John? How can I help?"

"It is the special education students. They are driving me absolutely nuts! They want to be treated like normal students until something happens, and then they want special treatment."

Mrs. Walker looked at him for a moment, weighed his anger, and then spoke in a sympathetic tone: "John, I understand your feelings. I know that teaching is sometimes difficult at best. I know that adding special education students to your classes has not been easy for you and some of the other teachers. But John, you are an excellent teacher, and you know that excellent teachers take students from where they

59

are and attempt to move them forward. Students are students. Of course, some are better and some can be problems. But it is up to you to do the best you can. I know that you are too good to let a problem like this get the better of you."

"Mrs. Walker, I did not spend four years in college to be a special education teacher; I spent my time learning how to be an English teacher. I know nothing about special education students, and after today I want to know even less!"

"What exactly transpired in your classroom that upset you?"

"One of the special education students, for no apparent reason, attacked one of my students and began to swear and hit him. I yelled for him to stop, but he would not. I finally had to physically separate the two boys. When I asked why this had occurred, the special education student said that he had been picked on. I suspended him from my class for fighting, and he told me that he was 'special education' and I could not do that. I am sick of these students wanting to be normal until something happens."

Mrs. Walker could feel the anger rising in herself. She fought for self-control as she said, "John, you are too good in the classroom to have said what you just did. All of the students are your students as long as they are in your classroom and under your direction. Special education students should be treated fairly, equally, and according to their ability. They have the same rights and expectations as everyone else. It is unfortunate that the myth of being a special education student and being exempt from rules and discipline seems to always be with us. If the student attacked without provocation, then that student will be disciplined whether or not he is in special education. I suggest you investigate further to see if he was, in fact, provoked."

Discussion Questions

1 Why do many teachers and administrators feel uncomfortable in dealing with special education or handicapped students?

2 Why did John Burns think of the special education student in a different manner than the other students who are in his class?

3 Did Mrs. Walker use the right approach when dealing with the teacher's frustration?

4 Should all teachers and administrators have training in dealing with special needs students who might be in their buildings or classrooms?

5 Why is it so easy for some teachers and administrators to forget the fairness issue when dealing with "different" students?

6 Should colleges spend more time teaching potential teachers and administrators the importance of using fairness, dignity, and respect in the classroom and in the school setting?

PERFORMANCE OBJECTIVE

THE ADMINISTRATOR FACILITATES
PROCESSES AND ENGAGES IN
ACTIVITIES ENSURING THAT
—All individuals are treated with fairness,
  dignity, and respect.

Case Study 24

A high number of discipline referrals have been written and processed at Community High School this quarter. In addition, more than the usual number of parent/guardian complaints have been heard. Moreover, the principal senses declining morale in the building; teachers seem to complain more about students and their difficulties teaching them. Brash behavior is sometimes expected from high school students struggling to mature, but this administrator wants to meet problems head on and avoid major difficulties later on. "We used to have a Courtesy Committee when I was in high school," he relates to his assistant. "What's wrong here? What has happened to treating others fairly, with dignity and respect?"

Discussion Questions

1 How might the principal ascertain that there are, indeed, problems in terms of members of the school community treating one another as they should? Can referrals, phone calls home, and morale be quantified? How would you advise the principal to study the problems?

2 Can standards be established, guidelines that ensure fair, dignified, and respectful treatment of all members of the school community? Why or why not? Explain your feelings.

3 In your own school district, how does the administration encourage fair, dignified, and respectful treatment of all members of the school community?

4 Would an outsider's school visits and perspective be more valuable in assessing the school's climate and morale? Is a survey necessary?

5 Suggest some possibilities, alternatives that might address the principal's concerns about fair, dignified, and respectful treatment of all members of the school community. Various schools have tried strategies that include:

- lectures by a psychologist, an expert in adolescent behavior, for faculty, staff, and students
- posting "Rules and Expectations" in every room of the school and in hallways; these include the behavioral norms that have been discussed in all classes
- revising a section of the student handbook to reflect the new objectives and expectations, listing consequences for infringement
- skits and short dramas staged by student council members illustrating a variety of common problems and solutions (verbally inappropriate insults, sexual innuendoes, comments about others' dress style, etc.)

Comments

Students often are removed from thinking about or discussing fair, dignified, and respectful treatment—until they, themselves, feel slighted or mistreated. Can faculty, staff and parent/guardians encourage students to be responsible in treating others well? How can this be done most effectively? What strategies work best, in your opinion, to gain student compliance? Is this not a problem for an individual classroom teacher on an "as needed, when the problem arises" basis? Some might argue that students naturally mature, growing out of unacceptable behavior that is basically an attention-getting mechanism. On the other hand, look at the television shows and the behavior of sports figures that students admire; their role models are not helping them understand and practice appropriate behavior, in many cases. How can anyone fight a barrage of poor examples of good behavior?

PERFORMANCE OBJECTIVE

THE ADMINISTRATOR FACILITATES
PROCESSES AND ENGAGES IN
ACTIVITIES ENSURING THAT
—Professional development promotes a
focus on student learning consistent with
the school vision and goals.

Case Study 25

By special arrangement with the management, a large amusement/ theme park just 40 minutes from most District 203 schools serves as the locale for the fall Teachers' Institute Day. This allows elementary, junior high and high school teachers to take part in a more comprehensive program since all participating schools share the expenses for nationally known speakers. This year's theme is "A School's Vision and Goals: Teaching and Learning for Tomorrow."

And yet the institutes are not always as successful as they could be, in the view of administrators. Many teachers bring student papers and grade during the presentations, or talk with others they are sitting near. Others assemble outside, sit on the benches, and eat the free apples; they miss the program offerings! Still others sign in, stand around long enough to spot building administrators and greet them, and then leave for the day. These individuals know where to park so that they can slip out easily. Administrators want better participation and attendance for the whole day, especially in view of the theme, the planning efforts, and the costs involved.

Discussion Questions

1 How can administrators guarantee faculty and staff attendance for the whole day's institute program? One school principal routinely insists that every professional on staff personally check in with the two deans in front of the main hall concession stand.

2 Attendance is one issue, but participation in individual sessions is also desired. What creates faculty involvement in inservice programs of this nature?

3 What steps can administrators take to prepare the faculty and staff in advance for inservice institutes and special programs? Should administrators preview program options, for example, or pick interesting items from presenter biographies to be read aloud at a faculty meeting?

Comments

Every educator wants to keep current. Thus, administrators sustain teachers' interest in professional development programs by inviting well-known experts and focusing on recent legislation, trends, and issues. Also, faculty and staff members may need to participate, to share their experiences and continue the dialogue related to their district, the school philosophy, vision, and mission. Allow faculty and staff members to serve on the program planning committees. Isolate topics of interest and encourage all teachers to respond to a survey-questionnaire to highlight issues teachers want information about. Allow volunteers to "continue the dialogue" begun at institutes days—by speaking about their experiences or research on specific topics at every faculty meeting throughout the year. Plan for small-group sessions by department to apply speakers' ideas and insights to specific departments, the school, and its students. One mid-year general faculty meeting might target, department by department, how the mission, goals, and vision of the school are being met in each classroom.

PERFORMANCE OBJECTIVE

THE ADMINISTRATOR FACILITATES
PROCESSES AND ENGAGES IN
ACTIVITIES ENSURING THAT
—Students and staff feel valued and
  important.

Case Study 26

Neither the building principal nor the superintendent is a "people person" in this district. Rather, these professionals are gifted in their fields, dedicated and hard-working. Both are motivated individuals who prefer working behind the scenes rather than in the limelight. Neither would ever call attention to individual, personal efforts. They seem to be authority figures in the district. Both put in long hours, and they get their jobs done well. Are students and staff missing out by not having the glad-handed, outgoing, personal relations-oriented individuals at key positions in the district? Does a leader lead by voice, manner, and effulgence?

Discussion Questions

1 Is a school leader obligated to change his/her personality and style to accommodate others' expectations or needs?

2 What steps can administrators take to convey their priorities for students and their ongoing commitment to faculty and staff efforts? For example, availability during lunch hours, daily, is a good practice.

3 Review effective leadership skills, compiling a short list of "must-haves." Now describe two very successful and effective administrators from your own experience on paper, in list form. Use verbs and adjectives, as: works to achieve consensus, promotes group harmony, or leads by example. Then "rate" the two administrators in terms of the desired traits listed on your "effective leadership skills" profile. What conclusions can you draw from this exercise?

Comments

School leaders need to listen to all members of the school community. They must seek input and plan for opportunities for exchange of ideas. As they are committed to the educational program in the district, leaders emphasize the importance of the school's mission, goals and objectives—and the educational success of each student. Leaders encourage ownership of the school and participation in school events and activities.

PERFORMANCE OBJECTIVE

THE ADMINISTRATOR FACILITATES
PROCESSES AND ENGAGES IN
ACTIVITIES ENSURING THAT
—The responsibilities and contributions of
each individual are acknowledged.

Case Study 27

After some discussion with the faculty, Principal John Evans had selected seven community members and parents to serve with 13 teachers and administrators on a committee to improve the school. (The state had mandated the study and the inclusion of community members in the process.) Prior to the first meeting, Mr. Evans met with five of the teachers.

"Before we have our first meeting with everyone here, I thought I would call you five together and have you help me decide how to divide up this big project. If you have any ideas, this is the time to tell me."

"Well, John," Rex said, "I don't think we can depend on the parents taking a leadership role in this. They simply don't have the professional background or experience—nothing against them—they just don't. We need to have the professionals be in charge."

Joan answered, "Rex, if we let them think that is our attitude, they won't come back again, that's for sure. I think we have to have them share responsibilities. Also, even though we have 13 teachers on the committee, I think we should consider ourselves as a steering committee and involve all the faculty."

"I think Joan has a point," Principal Evans said. "Every member of the faculty will be involved, whether they are on the committee or not. How can we best get everyone involved and make them feel good about their involvement?"

Discussion Questions

1 What ways can you think of to organize the total faculty (of 60) and community members to deal with the school improvement project?

2 How can the committee take a leadership role and still involve everyone else on the faculty?

3 Recognizing that the community members may not have direct knowledge of school operations, philosophy, and priorities, how can they best be used in the project?

4 Do the community members (parents and non-parents) bring anything to the group that the teachers do not bring?

5 Is Rex correct that the leadership roles (in whatever form the project organization takes) should all go to teachers?

6 How can the principal and/or committee acknowledge the contributions of the different individuals during the project in order to maintain interest and progress?

7 At the conclusion of the project, how can individuals be acknowledged for their contributions?

PERFORMANCE OBJECTIVE

THE ADMINISTRATOR FACILITATES
PROCESSES AND ENGAGES IN
ACTIVITIES ENSURING THAT
—Barriers to student learning are identified,
   clarified, and addressed.

Case Study 28

Dr. Wagner met with the curriculum coordinating committee of his district and told them that he was dissatisfied with the current curricular offerings at all levels and in all subjects.

Mrs. Marshall, a long-standing member of the committee and chair of the foreign language committee, visibly bristled at the superintendent's comments. "I take exception to that comment, Dr. Wagner. I have been in this district as a teacher and a department head for more than a quarter of a century. I believe our course offerings are superb. Where else can one find third- and fourth-year Latin being taught as well as introductory Russian and Greek?"

Dr. Wagner had expected some disagreement and was not surprised by Mrs. Marshall's comments. "I know that you have worked hard in the foreign language department, and I know that you are proud of the courses and of your accomplishments. However, I submit to you and to your fellow committee members that we are dealing with a rapidly changing student population. If you look at your enrollment patterns, you will see enrollment declining in these preparatory courses. I further submit that our students must learn the basics in all of their courses and that we must introduce diversity into our content areas and meet the demands of our current clientele. We must have students who are comfortable with technology and, if we are doing our job, they will be able to compete in a global market.''

Wagner concludes, "We must reevaluate our courses, alter their content in terms of students' needs, and realign our curriculum starting at the elementary level and moving up through high school. I want our students to be proud of themselves, their scholarship, and their heritage. I want them to leave our schools with the knowledge that they are ready to compete. I want us to realistically deal with our changing population because, ladies and gentlemen, whether we like it or not, they are a reflection of our educational expertise.''

Discussion Questions

1 Do you think that Mrs. Marshall's goals are consistent with the changing needs of the student population?

2 Was Dr. Wagner correct in his proactive approach to realigning the entire K–12 curriculum?

3 Should the curricular changes have been implemented broadly, or should they have been implemented in a more conservative fashion?

4 Do you believe the curriculum coordinating committee shared Dr. Wagner's vision for the school district clientele?

5 How do you perceive the coordinating committee and the teaching staff reacting to Dr. Wagner's proposals for curricular changes?

6 Are Mrs. Marshall's comments typical? How would you deal with her type of reasoning?

PERFORMANCE OBJECTIVE

THE ADMINISTRATOR FACILITATES
PROCESSES AND ENGAGES IN
ACTIVITIES ENSURING THAT
—Barriers to student learning are identified,
  clarified, and addressed.

Case Study 29

For a large number of Community High School students, part-time work during the week and on weekends is a reality. Many allow jobs to take precedence over schoolwork. Teachers are starting to complain to administrators and counselors about students not completing homework assignments or, worse yet, falling asleep in class. Some students have even verbalized that they had to "work late last night." Many parents support their children's jobs because working gives young people a sense of responsibility as it allows them to save money for college or maintain their own transportation. Besides, some parents reason, working keeps them out of trouble. One honor student has been so valuable to the salvage company he works for that he has become a night supervisor. This means he will not be able to participate in athletics this year, and the coach is beside himself since the young man possesses outstanding capabilities, is a team player, and inspires others to excel. He has already dropped band. In this community, few families are wealthy enough to fund higher education for their children, and yet most are ineligible for scholarships. This is a lower-middle and middle-income community whose members value work and jobs, as well as getting an education.

Discussion Questions

1 Should teachers alter their expectations, lowering their standards, when students are overburdened with school responsibilities and full work loads after classes?

2 Do counselors have an obligation to provide sessions for teachers regarding warning signs for students with problems? Students who assume work responsibilities outside school may have more serious problems than falling asleep in classes and dropping activities. They are at risk for depression when under pressure to succeed at both school and work, and they are missing out on their own high school years.

3 What steps can the school district take to involve students, parents/ guardians, and local businesses in dialogues about a problem that

only seems to be growing worse? What is the ideal ''balance'' of school and work for students?

4 Might the student/new night supervisor be released from some academic programs to do the salvage work as an intern, receiving school course credits?

Comments

Students need an adequate education in order to pursue higher education and prepare for careers. It is appropriate to encourage students to handle multiple responsibilities, and yet their first job is to take care of themselves. Students also have an obligation to excel in school. Do some students, however, mature before others and reveal a readiness to blend school and work responsibilities? On the other hand, is employment ever as important as education for young adults?

PERFORMANCE OBJECTIVE

THE ADMINISTRATOR FACILITATES
PROCESSES AND ENGAGES IN
ACTIVITIES ENSURING THAT
—Diversity is considered in developing
  learning experiences.

Case Study 30

For the new assistant principal, the high school and its community setting is a startling change of locale. This A.P. formerly worked in a well-known, well-respected suburban high school in which everyone subscribed to students' academic and social success. It was a wonderful place to work and to learn. Just a few hours away from that school is this one, and it seems to be a world away in terms of the differences. For one thing, the community's socioeconomic level is well below that of the previous suburb. The building is old, and many facilities are dated. Also, the student body boasts a diversity very much like urban downtown schools. Parent/guardians seem to work odd shifts (this is an industrial and manufacturing area in which several factories offer jobs; these are considered extremely desirable). When called, they are sometimes noticeably annoyed with their children's problems, almost belligerent. It is more like "It's your job to teach them and educate them for good jobs."

The school's noise level is also well above what the A.P. feels is acceptable; students seem rowdy, if not undisciplined, in the hallways. There are more discipline reports generated in one month here than in an entire semester at the suburban school. Students do not seem to respect the building as they should; for example, one teacher, quite dismayed, recently reported that a classroom bookcase had been damaged beyond repair. The school climate seems to reflect the anxiety of the students: roughly 12% do not graduate. Teachers want to put in their work time and go right home.

Discussion Questions

1 How can the A.P. take positive steps to change the climate/atmosphere of the school? In terms of your own experience, what initiatives make a difference to teachers and students? (Consider these: school motto, planned special event and assembly days, electives week, guest speakers, and theater group presentations).

2 Are there ways to involve the parent/guardians in their young adults' education? Note: These are busy people struggling to make ends meet. They may tend to view the school as one big bureaucracy, almost a hostile environment with well-educated faculty and staff members who may seem "above" them, not on their level. Suggest some starting points for involvement, for welcoming parent/guardians.

3 Without patronizing all of the diverse multicultural groups that make up the student body, can administrators pursue programs that will engender respect among all groups? It is important that students learn to get along and appreciate cultural differences. Should school-wide programs be established? How about discussions in a variety of classes? Lectures?

4 Students may learn to respect one another if getting along and communicating are the focus of routine classroom work. Might the A.P. initiate dialogues with the coordinator of curriculum studies about the prevalence and desirability of using panels, groups, open

discussions, and shared projects in as many classes as possible? How might one convince teachers to consider more activities requiring group dynamics? Can teachers include a new objective in their planning, something connected to recognizing and valuing diversity?

5 How might the A.P. understand in all its complexities the value systems of community members, parent/guardians, and students? A survey of opinions? Consulting local social service agencies? Inviting university sociology and psychology professors to study and describe the populace? Will understanding the community of the school lead to positive changes in the school and its offerings?

6 What specific programs encourage students to respect and value the uniqueness of the community, the school and its traditions, the importance of a solid educational base, and the exploration of a variety of job and career alternatives beyond high school?

PERFORMANCE OBJECTIVE
THE ADMINISTRATOR FACILITATES
PROCESSES AND ENGAGES IN
ACTIVITIES ENSURING THAT
—Diversity is considered in developing
  learning experiences.

Case Study 31

An irate parent phones the principal to complain about the emphasis her son Darryl's social studies teacher places upon students' understanding of various cultures throughout the world. "You've got sex education, healthy lifestyles units, gang information and prevention—and now *multiculturalism*! Enough already! Darryl goes to school to learn; he needs work in the basics, especially his understanding of mathematics." Darryl's mother knows about the district's strong commitment to teach young adults, but she is certain that school time spent on nonspecific skills units like multicultural education simply takes away time from academic study.

As the principal explains, students need to expand their view of the world and understand, if not appreciate, the rich traditions other cultures enjoy. ''This is a global village we live in. Workplace settings reveal multicultural work forces. Encouraging dialogue about differences among cultures may help students adjust to the ''real world'' once they graduate. We all need to be sensitized to other cultures.''

''This is America, you know,'' she comments. ''*E Pluribus Unum* and all that—the melting pot. English and mathematics should be taught in school. That's what will help these students get those jobs. And, you haven't heard the last from me.''

Discussion Questions

1 What other arguments might the principal use to convince Darryl's mother of the importance of making students multiculturally aware, if not multiculturally sensitive? Assume a wider perspective; is the focus on other cultures appropriate in some schools and not in others? Explain your perspective. Are schools responsible for making students aware of and sensitive to others? To what extent are they responsible?

2 Are special learning units and guest speakers appropriate in order to teach students about other cultures? How about a general review of historical milestones, traditions, festival days and celebrations worldwide? In other words, a very brief glimpse of some interesting cultures, with content selected by individual teachers. Comment upon cultural ''festivals,'' Asian-American Week, a Holocaust unit, etc.

3 How might school leaders help district teachers decide upon the degree of emphasis these units require?

4 How can teachers guard against the temptation to make multiculturalism activities synonymous with food festivals?

5 Would you advise a district to explain the emphasis on sensitizing students to various cultures in news features via the local newspaper? How can districts make parents and guardians aware of the importance of multicultural awareness, since these lessons must be reinforced in home settings?

6 Explain your district's emphasis on multiculturalism and recall what parameters are used to assess and evaluate the usefulness of the

learning units provided students. What other schools have programs that you feel are worthwhile related to this subject matter?

Comments

Schools change, as do programs. Textbooks have been revised to accommodate new views of ourselves and others. The working world is now a global marketplace. Advances in technology are awe-inspiring, and schools have embraced computers as additional tools of learning. Is the case not the same with the *multiculturalism* topic? Still, students come to school for academic training. Can schools justify their attempts to make young people aware of and sensitive to other cultures? Or, should student exchange programs comprise the extent of a school's obligation and involvement?

PERFORMANCE OBJECTIVE

THE ADMINISTRATOR FACILITATES
PROCESSES AND ENGAGES IN
ACTIVITIES ENSURING THAT
—Lifelong learning is encouraged and
   modeled.

Case Study 32

The principal of the high school felt that it would be helpful for the community to use school facilities in the evenings for noncredit courses for adults. He wanted to approach the superintendent about having a program that would offer things like typing, computers, some sports, maybe foreign languages, industrial arts courses, etc. On one hand, it would require more custodial time or a custodian to work a different shift, heat in the building during the evenings and air conditioning in the summer, perhaps more wear and tear on the building and equipment, and other factors. On the other hand, he could employ teachers to teach some of these classes and get them extra pay, and it would be good public relations for the school and the district.

Discussion Questions

1 What are other advantages and disadvantages besides those suggested by the principal?

2 If you were the principal, in what way would you approach the superintendent: a formal written presentation, a discussion, a note to see if there is any interest?

3 From the superintendent's viewpoint, are there considerations that you would have that are different from those of the principal?

4 Assume that the superintendent and board have approved the project and told you, the high school principal, that you are in charge of the whole thing. "Just make it pay for itself and do not use school funds." What steps would you take in establishing the program? And, in what order would you do these things? Consider what you would do in the following areas: publicity; payment to teachers (how much? how is the amount determined?); courses to offer; registration procedures; charges for courses; limitations on who can take courses, if any (resident of area, restricted to certain ages, like post-high school age); where to keep money received and the person who would account for it; minimum class membership before canceling; etc.

PERFORMANCE OBJECTIVE

THE ADMINISTRATOR FACILITATES
PROCESSES AND ENGAGES IN
ACTIVITIES ENSURING THAT
—Lifelong learning is encouraged and
  modeled.

Case Study 33

R. L. Buser, superintendent of District 203, is a career educator and has coined the phrase "Lifelong Learning: Let It Begin with District 203." Buser wants to inspire administrators and teachers, hoping to create a yearly program of interesting new opportunities for students. These are not necessarily connected to classroom activities. Teachers are confused.

At the faculty meeting where the idea is introduced, the English teachers, of course, are gung-ho. It is easy for them to start creative writing/creative visual arts magazines and writing contests by inviting in local authors and interested community people. They're out there in droves since it is a university town. Similarly, the English department has held several very successful spring Book Fairs. The local library contributed used books, and a distributor brought in boxloads of paperbacks. But how do the other departments and teachers respond to the challenge? Granted, there are teachers with specialty interests in the building; for example, one teacher is a member of the Audobon Society, another goes on archeological digs, and another is a skilled wood carver. However, where do departments begin?

Discussion Questions

1 What lifelong learners do you know whom you would like to serve as examples for students? Might this be a starting point for District 203; that is, identifying individuals who illustrate their dedication to continuing to learn?

2 Are electives and/or special electives weeks an alternative to consider? After all, Sports Week at the end of the school year is always a success. Or is that different?

3 How might an administrator create interest among departments and encourage teachers to participate in the effort to model and give examples of lifelong learning? What types of activities are possible?

4 Community members have talents and abilities, and there are many special interest groups in the area. Would they be interested in participating in the school's efforts? What community special interest/service groups might administrators and teachers immediately call upon for help? In some communities, the local gardening club and the arts and crafts guilds are noteworthy in their efforts.

5 Other than leaving course catalogues and brochures for students, how can community colleges and the local university encourage students to investigate the opportunities they offer?

Comments

A commitment to encourage lifelong learning is a challenge and an opportunity for schools. Students tend to see adults in academic settings in one-dimensional ways. Programs that allow faculty, staff, administrators, and community members to show the results of their skills, interests, hobbies, and abilities spark interest in students and, possibly, create new areas for them to explore. Inviting local authors to talk about their works is just the tip of the iceberg, so to speak. It targets a narrow range of students. Many students, on the other hand, respond to hands-on learning, experiments, building and design projects, and a host of other possibilities. Administrators and faculty need to start with specifics in terms of the talented people in the building and in the communities; they also need to consider a structure or forum in which these talents can be showcased.

PERFORMANCE OBJECTIVE

THE ADMINISTRATOR FACILITATES
PROCESSES AND ENGAGES IN
ACTIVITIES ENSURING THAT
—There is a culture of high expectations for
  self, student, and staff performance.

Case Study 34

Although the principal realizes that nurturing a culture of high expectations requires careful planning over a period of time, this administrator is motivated to start the process immediately. She lists some ideas that will hopefully draw the attention and involvement of every member of the school community. She is especially interested in targeting student efforts—improvements in academic achievement, increased service to school and community, renewed commitment to respect for others, and noticeable changes in what she terms "daily social courtesies." But the principal also wants to encourage staff members to strive for excellence in classroom instructional efforts. She does not exempt herself, realizing that she, above all, must model new behaviors.

She considers these changes a start toward creating the new climate of excellence:

- A "Student Good News" recognition column will appear in all district newsletter issues this year; the column will highlight student efforts in academic, social, and service areas. She will seek input from teachers in every department, schoolwide.
- A "Teacher Spotlight" column with appropriate graphics will also appear in the newsletter issues, with lists of the workshops and conferences teachers have attended. She, herself, will obtain quotes from the teachers about the value of these. Also, department chairpersons will be asked to write paragraphs on teachers whose instructional efforts extend beyond the ordinary and deserve recognition, if not emulation.
- Emphasizing the school's tradition of excellence can be brought to the students' attention via guest speakers at class assemblies and in academic classes. The principal will invite graduates representing many age levels to talk to students about their experiences during high school and after graduation. Interested members of the business community who have remained in the area will be also contacted.
- A year-long program of inservice staff development that focuses on continued professional growth and excellence in instructional services can be implemented; small groups will meet once a month during the year to follow up commitments to improvement. The theme of "effective strategies for enriching current instruction and programs" appeals to the principal.
- Attendance at special workshops on all aspects of educational leadership given during national and state conventions will be one area the principal will investigate. She will attend the workshops. In addition, she plans to set up classroom visitations, deciding to visit every single class in every department of the school this year. In view of the fact that she reads the *NASSP Bulletin,* she also decides to order four recent books recommended by that publication; she chooses two on effective leadership practices, one on reform efforts and TQM, and another on business management essentials. She also will review the nearest university's course offerings in the department of educational administration; she realizes a summer session may be more practical in terms of her schedule.

Discussion Questions

1 By what means and measures can an administrator assess a school's culture and expectations, including the nature of challenges posed for school leaders, teachers, and students? Can one conduct a survey, for example? An informal, unscientific poll? Hire an outside consultant? Accept volunteers for a subcommittee to study the issue? Is such an assessment necessary before creating new structures to change the status quo?

2 Review the value of meeting one single objective as opposed to attempting to make multiple changes geared toward increased expectations for one's own professional growth, the staff at large, and all students. Note: How might an administrator choose one single objective when so many changes are necessary?

3 Explain how a school leader might evaluate the success of efforts directed toward the principal's goal of creating high expectations. Does one need to consider evaluation strategies in planning new efforts? What evaluative measures might you suggest, given a goal that you believe is a particularly important one, related to the principal's targets?

4 Specify successful efforts you have witnessed, planned, been a part of, or know about related to a school district's efforts to create a "culture of high expectations."

5 If anything were possible, what types of efforts would you design and implement to meet the objective of creating a culture of high expectations for administrators, professional staff members, and students?

Comments

The principal's informal plans and notes, her attempts to create a climate of success and high expectations, are laudable and may well be necessary for her school. Has she, however, listed too many changes for the coming year? This is only a planning list; she admits it is "just a starting point" that she intends to expand.

PERFORMANCE OBJECTIVE

THE ADMINISTRATOR FACILITATES
PROCESSES AND ENGAGES IN
ACTIVITIES ENSURING THAT
—Technologies are used in teaching and
learning.

Case Study 35

John Rodgers, a superintendent-principal of a small K–12 school district, had just come back from a technology conference where he became excited about some of the new uses of technology for schools. He put this topic on the agenda for his next teachers' meeting for discussion. Part of the meeting went as follows:

"Mr. Rodgers, I understand your excitement about these new things, but most of us have not seen them. I know they cost a lot of money. Are they worth the cost? What difference will they make?"

Before Mr. Rodgers could answer Nancy's question, Don stated, "My concern is with the time it would take to learn how to operate any new technology and how I would incorporate it into the curriculum that I teach."

"A question I would like to ask is, 'What are we talking about?' " said Jennifer. "Do you mean computers or this Internet stuff I hear about all the time, or what? You know, we have a couple of old projectors that do not work too well. Maybe they are too low-tech to worry about."

Discussion Questions

1 It appears that Mr. Rodgers is a little more excited about the prospect of getting some new technology than his teachers. How would you answer Nancy's question about whether technology can make a difference in the ways teachers teach and in the ways that students can learn? Can you give some specific examples where technology can help teachers do a better job? Can technology help students learn better?

2 What are some of the technologies that Mr. Rodgers may be talking about? It appears that he was not very specific. Are they all equally effective?

3 Nancy also has a good point about costs. We do not have any information about Mr. Rodgers' district, but some technological advances do require a great deal of money. What is the situation in your own district? Has money been spent on technology? How did the district budget for these expenses? Are there substantial maintenance and upgrade costs to consider?

4 Don asked about the problem of learning to use new technology. How could you answer his question? How could you train teachers if they currently have no knowledge about computers, about the Internet, about presentation software, and about projection devices that hook up to computers and the Internet?

5 Would Mr. Rodgers need to hire someone to help the teachers daily with technology problems, equipment breakdowns, and training? Is this feasible in such a small district? Has your district employed such a person? If so, what are the job requirements and duties?

6 When would teachers be trained? Can you expect teachers to stay after school (or come evenings) for such training? Can you think of ways to encourage training, other than paying teachers extra money?

7 Don also asked about integrating technology into the current curriculum or revising the curriculum. How could you answer this question?

8 Jennifer made the point that some current equipment, once thought to be important technological equipment, is in need of repair. Is this a problem—that a district will spend money on the current technology and ignore repairs of things like overhead or movie projectors?

Comments

Administrators like Mr. Rodgers need to be aware of concerns such as those voiced by the teachers. The new technology is costly and often needs repairs by specialists. Also, the equipment is complex, and teachers have to be trained to use it. This training takes time, and it takes people who really know how to use it to do the training. Finally, administrators must demonstrate to teachers that the new technology makes a difference. What a waste it would be to purchase equipment, not have adequate training, not have someone to help the teachers, and not have the teachers realize how they can use it to improve instruction.

PERFORMANCE OBJECTIVE

THE ADMINISTRATOR FACILITATES
PROCESSES AND ENGAGES IN
ACTIVITIES ENSURING THAT
—Student and staff accomplishments are
  recognized and celebrated.

Case Study 36

The superintendent wanted each of his four high school principals to find a way to honor outstanding teachers. All four principals decided to ask the faculty in each school to select one of their own as Outstanding Teacher for the year. After the selection, each principal would find a way to honor that person: Give them an award, give them a reserved parking spot with their name on it, hold an assembly, or do something similar, though not necessarily the same in each building. Three principals found some way to have a person selected or elected by their respective faculty. However, the fourth called the superintendent and said, "You remember that we were going to find a way to honor an Outstanding Teacher this year? Well, I was really surprised. I mentioned this at a faculty meeting last week and received a petition today. Let me read it to you: 'After our faculty meeting last week, many of us have discussed your proposal that we select one of our teachers to be the Outstanding Teacher for this year. We do not like this idea and will not do it. We, signing below, believe that WE ARE ALL OUT-STANDING TEACHERS! No one of us is any better (or any worse) than the others in the building. So, since we are all outstanding, we cannot pick just one person.' Then, just about all of them signed their names. Isn't that something! They think they are equally good and won't pick one person from the building. What should I do? Should I pick someone or what?"

Discussion Questions

1 What would you tell this principal? Should he pick someone himself?

2 Why would teachers take such a position? Why did the teachers in the other three buildings go along willingly with the idea?

3 Could this principal have presented the matter differently to his faculty than the way the other principals presented it?

4 Is it wrong to pick one outstanding person from a group to be honored?

5 It makes sense to try to honor good teachers in some way. How would you honor these teachers in a way different than that attempted in this district?

PERFORMANCE OBJECTIVE

THE ADMINISTRATOR FACILITATES
PROCESSES AND ENGAGES IN
ACTIVITIES ENSURING THAT
—Student and staff accomplishments are
  recognized and celebrated.

Case Study 37

About a month after the superintendent in the previous case study had discussed the Outstanding Teacher concept, the board decided to get into the act. One board member stated that the district should honor all employees who had been there 5, 10, 15, etc., years by having them come to a board meeting some evening for special recognition. A second board member said this was a great idea but they should also invite all athletic teams that won conference championships, to which a third member added that nonathletic teams should also be invited. The board became excited about this concept and decided to ask all four principals to invite all of these people on the same night so that the board could congratulate them together. The press would be urged to be present. It would be a great night for the district.

Discussion Questions

1 As superintendent or principal, how would you react? What would you say or advise?

2 How much of an honor is it for a freshman girl, a 5-year teacher, or a 20-year custodian to shake hands with board members on a school night? How could you convey this to the board, or is it better not to say anything?

3 As principal, how would you approach each of these groups to explain the board's "honor night"?

4 As superintendent, how would you best structure the meeting that night? Who would you recognize and in what order? What about other board agenda items that legally must be handled that night? What suggestions would you make to the president for this meeting?

5 How could you, as superintendent, evaluate the night fairly and discuss the evaluation with the board so that they can plan for any future honors night?

PERFORMANCE OBJECTIVE

THE ADMINISTRATOR FACILITATES
PROCESSES AND ENGAGES IN
ACTIVITIES ENSURING THAT
—Multiple opportunities to learn are available
to all students.

Case Study 38

The principal, Bill Myers, was visiting a class taught by Walter Smith. Afterwards, Bill said to Mr. Smith, "I noticed that almost all of the time you stood behind the desk and lectured the students about the subject you were covering. From what I have seen in the past, that seems pretty typical of your style. Am I right?"

Walter replied, "Probably. My feeling is that I have to get this information across to them. If I do it this way, I am always looking at them, making sure the class is paying attention. And, I can check my notes to make sure I don't miss anything. I don't just read notes to them, you know. Also, I don't see the sense in asking them to tell me things, because they have never taken this subject before, so they can't be expected to know it. It's my job to teach them and their job to listen and learn the material. What's wrong with that?''

Discussion Questions

1 Is anything wrong with that?
2 Mr. Myers feels that some students might learn very well from Mr. Smith's method, but that other students might not learn as well. What do you think?
3 If you feel that different students learn in different ways (or maybe the same person learns in different ways in different circumstances), what other ways are there?
4 What can Mr. Myers do to encourage Mr. Smith to consider other approaches? Is it helpful for him to have Mr. Smith visit other teachers who use other styles?
5 Does it make any difference what the subject matter is? In other words, do some classes lend themselves to certain styles of teaching more than others?
6 This case study deals with multiple opportunities to learn, based on different teaching/learning styles, within a single classroom. How can the school as a whole offer its students a variety of opportunities to learn?

PERFORMANCE OBJECTIVE

THE ADMINISTRATOR FACILITATES
PROCESSES AND ENGAGES IN
ACTIVITIES ENSURING THAT
—The school is organized and aligned for
  success.

Case Study 39

District 134 administrators look forward to the completion of the summer construction and improvement projects as a way to update the senior high building. A recent addition to the staff, a well-qualified curriculum director, should also ensure that course content and programs are aligned with revised goals and objectives in the district. The principal is most concerned about the fact that John J. Willard High School is regarded among students as "the prison" and that faculty and staff there seem tired, if not pessimistic. "There's no spirit at Willard any more," one administrator comments to another. "I wish we could change things so that everyone looked forward to coming to work here; it would be wonderful to have students *enjoy* learning and what the school offers them. Well, the building projects, the painting, and the new C.D. will make the difference and turn things around."

Discussion Questions

1 Is the principal correct in assuming that the construction projects, painting, and a new curriculum director will change the atmosphere, if not the climate, in the building? What elements create a school's atmosphere? What are the most desirable qualities that characterize an effective school, one that is organized and aligned for success? (some might include openness, optimism, excitement, a pleasant place filled with opportunities).

2 Give the principal some advice. How does an administrator pinpoint other changes necessary to improve the building atmosphere, change the climate, and alter the attitudes of students and staff toward school? How can one begin a program to change attitudes? How can one encourage everyone in the school community to work toward new goals?

3 What does the organization of the school have to do with success? Are some organizational structures better than others? Do some lead to success more easily? If so, what kinds?

Comments

Administrators, especially principals, help establish and set the tone of the school building. There is often a delicate balance to maintain—openness but also structured experiences geared toward the best education possible for young people. How does one maintain the balance? How can administrators let everyone know that things will change at school? Note: Some schools hold sport days, fall bonfires, dress-down days, all-day electives in which every member of the school community participates (i.e., crafts demonstrations, art shows, and similar offerings), special guest speakers and special program days, and even contests for a new school slogan/motto/logo. One school in Indiana sells senior students parking lot spaces that the students can decorate by painting. Changing the atmosphere and climate of a building requires a fundamental rethinking of what the goals are and how to change things to accommodate the new way of viewing the school and its students.

PERFORMANCE OBJECTIVE

THE ADMINISTRATOR FACILITATES
PROCESSES AND ENGAGES IN
ACTIVITIES ENSURING THAT
—Curricular, cocurricular, and extracurricular
   programs are designed, implemented,
   evaluated, and refined.

Case Study 40

Jake Snowman, a board member, read from an article in *Businessman's Weekly* to the other board members at the regular April board meeting. This article stated that new hires had very little knowledge of "practical" usage of mathematical concepts in business. After reading a few paragraphs, Jack added, "This is what I have been saying for some time. The people I hire, right out of our own high school, cannot do percentages to figure out discounts or even their own commissions. And, we have a really hard time finding graduates who can work in our office if the work involves budgets, simple accounting, inventory control, and other areas like that. I think we should take a good look at our mathematics program, especially for those students who will be going to work when they graduate from high school, and design the program so that our students will do better on the job."

After some discussion by the board members and the superintendent, who described what the district was doing currently, the board passed a motion to have the superintendent meet with the appropriate personnel and redesign the mathematics program for the non-college-bound students. The superintendent was to report back to the board at the September board meeting.

Discussion Questions

1 First of all, do you believe that a board would ever pass motions like the one referred to above?

2 As superintendent, who would you consult on this program design? Who should be involved? Who should be in charge of the project?

3 For the design component, who should be involved? Only mathematics teachers, or teachers from other departments? Should any nonschool people be involved? If so, from what area, and what can they contribute? Is there any reason to talk to other school districts or university personnel?

4 Once the people have been assembled, what steps should be taken to design the new mathematics curriculum? What timelines might be considered?

5 For the implementation component, one teacher suggests that the new curriculum be run as a pilot program in one building. What are the advantages and disadvantages of this proposal? How should you choose the teachers for the new program? Does it matter which people are chosen? Should the program be restricted to "math classes" and "math teachers," or should other areas in the school curriculum be involved in implementing the program?

6 For the evaluation component, what would you suggest in order to evaluate how the program is going? If a pilot program were established, how can this be used for evaluation? If student testing is a part of the process, how can it be used to help evaluate the new program? Does it help with evaluation that some students may be taking the "old" mathematics program alongside the pilot program? Besides this quantitative evaluation, what qualitative evaluation could be done and with whom?

7 For the refinement component, what process would you suggest in order to make recommendations to improve the program? Who should be involved in this process? When should this component take place?

8 Once all of the above components have been discussed and conclusions have been agreed to, how would you structure the presentation to the board at the September board meeting?

PERFORMANCE OBJECTIVE

THE ADMINISTRATOR FACILITATES
PROCESSES AND ENGAGES IN
ACTIVITIES ENSURING THAT
—Curriculum decisions are based on
research, expertise of teachers, and the
recommendations of learned societies.

Case Study 41

Mary Martell was the principal of a high school. During the past several weeks, several curriculum questions had come across her desk, and teachers were mentioning the importance of changing some of the curriculum. With this in mind, Mary spoke to her Principal's Advisory Committee, a committee of teachers elected from the faculty.

"I want to get your advice about how we should look at our curriculum and make curriculum decisions in this building. I note that there are several important decisions coming up this next semester, and I am sure we will have more in the future."

"Mary, I think it is best to have curriculum decisions made at the department level by the teachers who deal with it daily," stated one teacher in mathematics.

"Well, I hate to disagree," said a history teacher," but departments cannot make these decisions in isolation of each other. What one department does often affects the curriculum of another department—or at least it should affect them. I would favor curriculum decisions made by the Department Chair Council when it meets with Mary."

"I'll give you another view," said the English teacher. "What we could do is establish a curriculum committee, composed of elected 'curriculum experts' from each department and some parents, students, and administrators. This committee could look at the high school curriculum from the 'big picture' angle and make decisions that are best for the whole school, not just for a department. And, Mary, if it helps you, we could have their decisions be recommendations to you for the final decisions.''

A science teacher looked around the table and stated, ''I don't know what is wrong with this group making curriculum decisions or any decisions for that matter. We are elected from all departments. We could just discuss curriculum decisions in these meetings and vote right here.''

Mary thanked them for their ideas and said she would get back to them at the next meeting. She went on to the next agenda item.

Discussion Questions

1 Consider each of these options. What are the advantages and disadvantages of each?

2 Which option seems to be best for the school as a whole?

3 Which option might have the best curriculum people involved? the least expertise involved?

4 Does a school really need a formal curriculum decision-making group other than individual teachers?

5 Do curriculum decisions really affect more than one department? If you think so, give specific examples of how this could happen. Is this important? If so, which option suggested in the case study would be best in considering the impact of decisions on other departments for this factor?

6 How does your school make curriculum decisions? Is it a better way than these options? Which of these options would work well at your school?

7 Can you think of options not named above that are better than those named?

PERFORMANCE OBJECTIVE

THE ADMINISTRATOR FACILITATES
PROCESSES AND ENGAGES IN
ACTIVITIES ENSURING THAT
—The school culture and climate are
  assessed on a regular basis.

Case Study 42

School culture can include many things. One thing is the nickname chosen for the athletic teams. This case study relates a real incident that happened to a new superintendent. Dr. Trenton came from a large suburban school to a small midwest town, Pekin, Illinois. At Dr. Trenton's former school, the nickname given to the teams was associated with a wild animal, but the Pekin teams had, for many years, been known as the Pekin Chinks. One of the first things Dr. Trenton said was that the nickname must be changed. Years ago, no one discussed whether names like *Indians* and *Redmen* were appropriate, but today many feel that these names should not be used.

Dr. Trenton felt that the name *Chinks* was a derogatory term for Chinese and should be changed. The school's mascot was a drawing of a Chinese character with slanted eyes in old Chinese clothing. Many in the community felt that the name had been used for many years with no complaints. There was no intention, they stated, to make fun of anyone. It was just a nickname the school adopted years ago.

Discussion Questions

1 What about timing? Should the superintendent have waited for several months or a year before approaching this topic, or was it better that he attack it from the beginning?

2 Do you think the name and logo should be changed? Can you see good arguments from a viewpoint different than your own?

3 Have we become too sensitive today about issues like this that no one noticed for many years?

4 Can you think of any compromise that might be acceptable to the community and to the superintendent?

5 How will this position—having nothing to do with academics—affect other aspects of the superintendent's job and relationships?

6 If you were Dr. Trenton and felt as strongly as he did, what steps would you take to change the name? Who should be consulted and in what order should he talk to them?

7 Assuming that it is agreed that a new name is to be chosen, who should choose it? What process should be used to choose the name?

8 With such controversy in many towns with many teams, is it necessary to have *any* nickname and logo? What about selecting a name that does not refer to anything or anyone? For example, Northwestern University considered, and rejected, *Purple Haze* a few years ago.

PERFORMANCE OBJECTIVE

THE ADMINISTRATOR FACILITATES
PROCESSES AND ENGAGES IN
ACTIVITIES ENSURING THAT
—The school culture and climate are
  assessed on a regular basis.

Case Study 43

Many years have passed and Dr. Trenton has decided that he wants to assess the climate of the school. A college professor met with him and discussed how he would survey a random sample of teachers, parents, and community members. He suggested using an instrument that he had developed to assess the climate of the school for those who work there. It would also include the climate of the school in the view of people in the community, especially those who had children in the district.

Dr. Trenton decided to save the money that would have been spent on the consultant's fee and do the study himself.

Discussion Questions

1 What advantages does the consultant have over Dr. Trenton in assessing the climate? Disadvantages?

2 Remembering the consultant's concepts, Dr. Trenton decided to do a random sample. Why is a random sample done? How would you choose a random sample of teachers? of parents? of community members (non-parents)? How many would you choose? Does it make any difference?

3 What questions would you ask? How would you come up with the questions? Would you use questions whose answers are yes/no, multiple-choice, or would you use open-ended questions requiring a written response?

4 How would you distribute the surveys? How would you collect them?

5 Once you get the surveys back, how would you tabulate the results and interpret them?

Comments

If Dr. Trenton does not have a good background in survey techniques and does not wish any expert advice, he had better obtain a book on this subject and read it prior to doing the survey. All of the points made above—the sample, the questions, the type of responses required, the distribution and collection of the survey, and the tabulation and interpretation of the results—are very important. In fact, if he ignores good survey technique in these areas, the results may be entirely incorrect or unrepresentative and lead to much confusion and debate. In other words, a poorly planned survey can negatively affect the school climate it just surveyed.

PERFORMANCE OBJECTIVE

THE ADMINISTRATOR FACILITATES
PROCESSES AND ENGAGES IN
ACTIVITIES ENSURING THAT
—A variety of sources of information is used
to make decisions.

Case Study 44

This case is one of five case studies (Case Studies 44–48), all involving Betty Johnson, the high school principal.

Betty Johnson, the high school principal, received a note from one or her teachers, Brad Carlton. It stated, ''I have talked to you about Marybelle before. She just won't pay any attention in class and keeps distracting others. I know you have talked to her, and I think her counselor talked to her about something last week, too, although I don't know if it was her behavior in my class. Anyway, I've had it. I have told Marybelle not to come back to my class. I don't want to see her again. The class will be better off without her. Please back me up on this.''

Discussion Questions

1 Where can Betty get additional information for that case, if it is available?

2 Should Betty make the decision alone or consult with others?

3 Can you think of one or more solutions to the problem?

PERFORMANCE OBJECTIVE

THE ADMINISTRATOR FACILITATES
PROCESSES AND ENGAGES IN
ACTIVITIES ENSURING THAT
—A variety of sources of information is used
　to make decisions.

Case Study 45

Mary, an English teacher at the high school, ran into Betty Johnson's office waving the class lists for the new year. ''Betty, do you know how many students the counselors have put into my second period class? Look at this—35 students! And I am supposed to have discussion in this class? Please make another section and divide the class up into two classes.''

Discussion Questions

1 Where can Betty get additional information for that case, if it is available?

2 Should Betty make the decision alone or consult with others?

3 Can you think of one or more solutions to the problem presented?

PERFORMANCE OBJECTIVE

THE ADMINISTRATOR FACILITATES
PROCESSES AND ENGAGES IN
ACTIVITIES ENSURING THAT
—A variety of sources of information is used
  to make decisions.

Case Study 46

Dan, the athletic director, called Betty on the phone. He said, "Our boys' basketball team just came back from the tournament—which they won, by the way. But, before they arrived back, I got two calls from store owners where they were playing. They said that some of our players came in bragging about how they had beaten their hometown team and took some candy and hats. Also, there are rumors that some of our players were drinking beer in the back of the bus. Our coach sits in the front. I have not talked to him yet as I thought I should talk to you first. I know that we have to do something. On the other hand, the school spirit is so high this year because of this team's record. What do you want me to do?"

Discussion Questions

1 Where can Betty get additional information for that case, if it is available?

2 Should Betty make the decision alone or consult with others?

3 Can you think of one or more solutions to the problem presented?

PERFORMANCE OBJECTIVE

THE ADMINISTRATOR FACILITATES
PROCESSES AND ENGAGES IN
ACTIVITIES ENSURING THAT
—A variety of sources of information is used
  to make decisions.

Case Study 47

"Mrs. Johnson," Betty's secretary said, "We just had a call from the Methodist Church wanting to use our multipurpose room this Sunday because of the fire they had this week. They want to hold church services here for several weeks at least. What should I tell them, or do you want to talk to them? As you know, the superintendent is on vacation."

Discussion Questions

1 Where can Betty get additional information for that case, if it is available?
2 Should Betty make the decision alone or consult with others?
3 Can you think of one or more solutions to the problem presented?

PERFORMANCE OBJECTIVE

THE ADMINISTRATOR FACILITATES
PROCESSES AND ENGAGES IN
ACTIVITIES ENSURING THAT
—A variety of sources of information is used
  to make decisions.

Case Study 48

"Mrs. Johnson, our son, Donald, just isn't learning in Mary's first period class. I know that Mr. Carlton's class has room, and I want Donald to be in his class. It's the same course and the same book, and Donald has a study hall that period, so the change should be easy to do."

Discussion Questions

1 Where can Betty get additional information for that case, if it is available?
2 Should Betty make the decision alone or consult with others?
3 Can you think of one or more solutions to the problem presented?

PERFORMANCE OBJECTIVE

THE ADMINISTRATOR FACILITATES
PROCESSES AND ENGAGES IN
ACTIVITIES ENSURING THAT
—Student learning is assessed using a
variety of techniques.

Case Study 49

Standardized tests, along with essay exams and multiple-choice tests created by teachers, are valid indicators of what students have learned. So are portfolio collections. However, teachers need to reach beyond these, so the school principal uses a faculty meeting to pose other alternatives. The principal suggests:

- single projects agreed upon by both student and teacher, projects requiring research (reading additional material and writing summaries of individual articles or chapters) or interviews with specialists or participation in additional classes
- creating a film or documentary, a TV news magazine feature, or a news article or feature story
- creating a computer game or project related to the objectives
- creating an artwork, musical selection, or model
- teaching another group of students, with the evaluating teacher observing and, perhaps, testing students when completed
- compiling an annotated bibliography related to the material
- creating several tests on the material
- creating a series of posters illustrated with tables, graphs, charts or diagrams, or handouts with sample problems related to the material
- outreach activities in the community—working with and in local businesses, community organizations, hospitals, churches, and service organizations

Discussion Questions

1 What other assessment strategies test student learning besides those listed above? Draw attention to projects, experiments, and other hands-on applications.

2 Is it legitimate for teachers to have students submit lists of ideas detailing how they, themselves, would be willing to show mastery of the unit goals and objectives? Note: Teacher and student would agree upon the contents and scope of a final assessment strategy.

3 What prevents nontest evaluations from becoming busy work or slap-dash efforts with no real substance?

4 Would a principal pressure teachers too much if he/she asked for single-page briefs at the end of each quarter that reviewed the nonpaper test alternatives used to assess learning in the classes of each teacher in the building? How might publishing lists of these alternative assessment strategies affect teachers? Might a portion of faculty meetings center on departmental alternatives, so that all teachers know there are viable choices available?

Comments

Actual paper-and-pencil tests are seldom a part of students' lives after secondary and postsecondary education. However, students must have experience in fulfilling goals and objectives with end-products in mind, tangible proofs of mastery learning. Students must also understand and apply their own skills, abilities and talents to all learning. Awareness of the goals and objectives, paired with one's own skills and talents, leads to practical applications. Similarly, consulting with business people in the community who may want to aid young people in their awareness of what activities are common to business operations is a connection to workplace responsibilities.

PERFORMANCE OBJECTIVE

THE ADMINISTRATOR FACILITATES
PROCESSES AND ENGAGES IN
ACTIVITIES ENSURING THAT

—Multiple sources of information regarding
  performance are used by staff and
  students.

Case Study 50

In the faculty lounge at the high school, several teachers were discussing the evaluation of their students. Here are some of their comments:

- "I give my students three exams a semester and average the three scores for their semester grade. It works out pretty well."
- "Well, I give several exams, too, but I also have a grade for homework and another for effort to average in with the exams."
- "I think it is important to assess performance all the time. Some students do not do well on big exams if you have only three a semester. So, I have a quiz at the beginning of the period every day, plus a short exam every Friday."
- "With all those quizzes and exams, I don't know how you have time to present any material! What I do is to have two or three exams each semester, plus a student project."
- "Last year I read about portfolios, so I require each student to keep a portfolio on everything that is done during the semester. They turn that in to be graded before each grading period."
- "I do that, too, but I also added something else. Each student has to make a formal presentation to a panel on some subject I approve. I invite school people that I know from other schools to serve on the panel and grade the students."

Discussion Questions

1 Do any of these evaluation methods coincide with your own?
2 Do you know of other teachers who use each of these methods?
3 Is one of these methods better than the others? Worse than the others?
4 Assume that you are the school principal. Which of these would be easiest for you to defend to a parent? Hardest to defend?
5 As the principal, which is easiest to defend to yourself? Hardest?
6 Is it important to have more than one type of performance by which to judge student achievement? Why or why not?

7 What are other methods that a teacher might employ, with the goal of using multiple ways for evaluation?

8 If you were a principal and a beginning teacher came to you to ask how to evaluate students, what would you say?

9 Are all the methods equally good for all high school subject areas? Are some methods better for some areas than others? If so, which methods and which areas?

10 How do you feel about dropping letter grades and giving students "grades" like "has mastered material" and "is still learning"?

PERFORMANCE OBJECTIVE

THE ADMINISTRATOR FACILITATES
PROCESSES AND ENGAGES IN
ACTIVITIES ENSURING THAT
—A variety of supervisory models is
  employed.

Case Study 51

At a general administrative meeting consisting of the superintendent, all principals, and all department chairs, as well as various directors and coordinators, the superintendent was discussing the need to do a good job in supervising their areas. One of the principals said, "When you started to talk about supervising this morning, I guess I was thinking about supervising and evaluating teachers. But it seems you mean a broader definition. Is that right?"

"Yes," the superintendent replied, "I am talking about all types of supervision. Some of you rarely even see a teacher, yet you have supervisory responsibilities in your area. What I would like each of you to do for our next meeting is to keep a journal of the various supervisory roles that you have and whether you use different models of supervision in each of those roles—or even different models within the same role. The reason why I am having you do this exercise is that there are different ways to supervise, and I think that, with the wide variety of experiences that are represented here, we will be able to discuss different models. In this way, some of you will learn about new models for you that may be quite appropriate in your position."

Discussion Questions

1 What are some reasons that a superintendent might want the administrative staff to do this exercise?

2 Does a person's supervisory style usually change naturally over time, or is it necessary to do something like this to cause some changes? Why is it beneficial to consider other models of supervision?

3 Are there any models of supervision that seem more appropriate for each administrative group (e.g., principals), or is it true that all administrators can use different models regardless of their positions?

4 Is it an advantage for different administrators to have different models, or is it better for all to share the same model?

5 One administrator later reported that he felt that he used the facilitator model of supervision. If true, what might he mean by that? What advantages and disadvantages are there if he uses this model for all his roles?

6 Another administrator said that his supervisory model could be compared to General Patton's: "I tell them what I expect and hold them to it." What are the advantages and disadvantages in this model?

7 Think of the different roles a principal plays, and make a list of those roles. What type of supervisory model would seem to be ideal for each of those roles?

8 How can administrators be trained to use models different than those they use now?

PERFORMANCE OBJECTIVE

THE ADMINISTRATOR FACILITATES
PROCESSES AND ENGAGES IN
ACTIVITIES ENSURING THAT
—Pupil personnel programs are developed to
  meet the needs of students and their
  families.

Case Study 52

The community high school administrative team members share concerns during their regular monthly meeting:

- A student in one conference school recently committed suicide.
- Several serious fights occurred on campus, requiring police intervention.
- Rumors are circulating about the availability of controlled substances in the vicinity of the tattoo parlor located only miles from school.

A variety of recommendations surface in their discussions; these include the following:

- An invitation to an adolescent-specialist psychiatric team to offer professional educators and parent/guardians perspectives about teen deaths and suicides. Approaches may include workshop-style small groups that will review causes, symptoms, and signs troubled teens may exhibit, as well as preventive measures to take. Recommendations for involving all district students and parent/guardians will be sought.
- An evening town meeting forum at the high school might review perspectives on violence from law enforcement and social service agency representatives as well as school officials. Antidotes to misbehavior, including establishing a teen drop-in/crisis center, opening selected school athletic facilities in the evening, and creating additional local community center programs for preteens and teens will be discussed and other ideas considered.
- Local law enforcement officials and social service agencies will be asked to create an ad campaign and present student assemblies and programs that stress anti-drug use, anti-alcohol consumption.
- Increased involvement of school security staff personnel, with the addition of personnel, will be sought as deemed necessary.

Discussion Questions

1 What parameters might school officials observe when utilizing groups from outside the school setting? For example, one district

has found that the more negative or heavy-handed the presentation, the less likely students respond. Similarly, distributing literature to students seems to have little effect, if any.

2 Will one well-publicized town meeting suffice for deterring violence? What specific suggestions (for example, research about this particular community's problems) can school leaders offer? What follow-up strategies are necessary?

3 How can school personnel elicit the cooperation and backing of students in their efforts, especially school leaders, members of sports teams, newspaper staff members, and other influential groups? Sometimes, a bandwagon effect is necessary.

4 Describe successful programs that you know about that address these and similar troubling contemporary realities affecting schools and students. Design a program you would like to see implemented targeting one specific problem.

Comments

Activities that are forbidden or appropriate only for adults often attract teens who are impressionable and struggling to realize their own identities. Parents may not be aware of how easy it is for students to circumvent rules and how appealing "living dangerously" is. Without appearing to champion "goody two-shoes" behavior, how can school administrators, parent/guardians, and community members set high standards and reveal the desirability of appropriate, responsible behavior? Are schools answerable when they neglect to assume more "parental" responsibilities in these areas?

CHAPTER 5

Standard 3 Case Studies

A school administrator is an educational leader who promotes the success of all students by ensuring management of the organization, operations, and resources for a safe, efficient, and effective learning environment.

PERFORMANCE OBJECTIVE

THE ADMINISTRATOR FACILITATES
PROCESSES AND ENGAGES IN
ACTIVITIES ENSURING THAT
—Knowledge of learning, teaching, and
student development is used to inform
management decisions.

Case Study 53

Decision-making is an important part of an administrator's responsibility. At Community High, the principal brainstorms with other building administrators and considers several potential problems that need discussing and, possibly, solutions. These include

- setting up an English lab and resource center so that students can receive individualized help from teachers during all periods of the day
- creating a pilot program integrating science skills in upper-division classes, which includes classes conducted at a corporation's research and development labs; a local corporation is interested in bridging the gap between school and work settings

- accommodating students' need for planning portfolio projects with teachers; can the current semester schedule allow extended class periods every other week for the second quarter?
- keeping class sizes "reasonable" to "small," a priority for some subject areas, but not for all
- checking to see whether all computers are operational and available for students and teachers
- determining whether teachers are trying new approaches with students, including planning with a variety of student learning styles in mind; considering whether an inservice session is enough to lead the way
- encouraging students to assume more responsibility for their own learning may create the need for independent study time outside the classroom

Discussion Questions

1 Is the principal on the right track in focusing decisions exclusively on increasing opportunities for students? Is it good to involve all administrators in this problem-solving?

2 What are various strategies to use to encourage board members to support these decisions and the extra costs added to the district budget?

3 How do administrators investigate what new research studies are available and relevant to the district's educational program? What is the place of research in school settings?

4 What guidelines for effective decision-making can you offer administrators? Won't all decisions that center on effective teaching, student learning, and development be appropriate management decisions? Explain why or why not, in terms of your answer to the last question posed.

5 How might administrators encourage teachers to incorporate computer applications in their learning units? What are the advantages of students and teachers exploring the Internet?

Comments

Management decisions start from a leader's perspective and anticipate the schoolwide ramifications when they involve educational
choices. Decisions related to learning, teaching, and student development (and changes in educational practices) often require modification
of existing structures. Knowing how to balance the managing of a
stable educational program with providing new opportunities requires
a set of parameters or guidelines.

PERFORMANCE OBJECTIVE

THE ADMINISTRATOR FACILITATES
PROCESSES AND ENGAGES IN
ACTIVITIES ENSURING THAT
—Operational procedures are designed and
  managed to maximize opportunities for
  successful learning.

Case Study 54

When the plans for Alexandria Junior/Senior High School were
presented to the school board by the architects, the board immediately
began to look for ways to cut costs from the project. They wanted to
have a new school that was what they considered to be state of the
art, but they felt the public would not stand for the costs involved.

"We want the most bang for the buck," said Mr. Bolton, president
of the board.

"I agree," echoed Mrs. Sinton, the newly elected board member.
The other five members nodded their heads in avid agreement. "We
cannot expect the taxpayers to fund this project at the costs you are
submitting."

At this juncture, Arnold Duke, the principal, leaned forward in his
chair and smacked his palm down upon the conference table. "I cannot
believe what you people are saying!" he exclaimed in a voice fraught
with anger. "You are thinking of your own reelection bids rather than
what is best for the students. You are wanting state of the art, but you
are not willing to fight the battle to obtain it."

"Now, Arnold," said Mr. Bolton solicitously, "you simply do not understand the larger picture. We have to watch the taxpayers' dollars. Do you think we really need all this computer technology and all the wiring and bells and whistles that go with it?"

"Mr. Bolton, I have been an educator for more than 30 years. I have dedicated my life to the betterment of the students in this district. We must have the educational facilities so that we can maintain and develop the educational programs of tomorrow. All of you on this board want what is best for students. I urge you to accept these plans so that our students can compete and so that they can have the best education that you—we—would want for our children."

Discussion Questions

1 How much input should boards of education have in the operational procedures of any school?

2 Do you agree with Mr. Bolton's concern about taxpayers' expenditures?

3 Do you believe Mr. Duke was out of line when he spoke so forcefully to the board of education?

4 How much input do you feel the principal of the school should have with regard to curricular offerings?

5 As a principal, how would you address the concerns of the board?

PERFORMANCE OBJECTIVE

THE ADMINISTRATOR FACILITATES
PROCESSES AND ENGAGES IN
ACTIVITIES ENSURING THAT
—Operational procedures are designed and
  managed to maximize opportunities for
  successful learning.

Case Study 55

During a faculty meeting early in the year, some specific teacher concerns surface. These include those listed below.

1 There is a suggestion that all students meet with adult "advisors" on a one-to-one basis; these adults from the teaching and professional staff will serve as trouble-shooters and counselors who maintain close contact with specific students all year long. Adults will monitor their progress, suggest study skills as needed, and listen to students if they wish to confide problems.

2 A concern about review and supplemental help in all academic classes seems advisable, especially for the sometimes overlooked "average" ability students and underinvolved students. Labs, workshops, and individual tutorial help should be available, in the view of many teachers.

3 Because students must complete research reports, projects, and term papers, they must understand the research process. "Hands-on" work is vital. Students need to be be able to find information from many sources. We are still in the middle of an "information explosion," some of which is virtually unknown to students.

4 English classes always seem too large to individualize learning. Consequently, students always meet as a big group. Nevertheless, many studies indicate that small groups are preferable; desired student involvement increases, as does interaction with others toward solving unit-specific problems. Discussion skills also increase. By comparison, lecture and individual practice become the norm with large classes, or so research studies indicate.

As administrators and teachers discuss these concerns, their commitment escalates; all want to change the school constructs to meet the needs of the students. Some interesting "answers" are considered. First, utilizing several schedule formats will allow everyone some flexibility; teachers are enthused about the prospect of meeting student advisees at least once a month in a single-period "open" advisory period option. On that day, Schedule B would be in effect, with shortened periods and open study areas available throughout the building for students who are waiting to see advisors.

Administrators and teachers also consider several "open" afternoons after lunch periods are over, or at least trying this once or twice. They seek to provide science enrichment units, increased drills and mastery in language labs, special subject-related tutorials, English resource centers and workshops, and a special math clinic that even includes student tutors who are gifted in mathematics.

Library and computer resources specifically geared to availability of research related to historical figures and key events in U.S. history are deemed useful. Extensive bibliographies must be compiled, but students will learn how to access information, with help from professionals. Teachers schoolwide agree that most of the research studies assigned for this year would center on social studies material, in view of the perceived weakness of students. It may be possible to invite librarians from the community college and the university to plan and organize this option.

The English teachers are adamant about creating stable "reference groups" of six students each in most of their classes; groups will be assigned to problem-solving, learning discussion techniques, and assuming much more responsibility for their own learning. Groups will help plan activities per unit, based on course and unit objectives. Their plans will include suggestions for the means to evaluate their learning. The teachers want the groups to meet in designated areas throughout the building, monitored by aides, volunteer teachers, or paraprofessionals. They feel the small additional investment necessary to compensate these adults is more than justified by what they are sure will result: increased student learning opportunities.

Discussion Questions

1 What is your opinion of these teachers' suggestions? Are these workable alternatives to perceived problems? What additional problems do you think will result if these options are pursued?

2 To what extent are the operational procedures of a school to be changed to maximize opportunities for what professionals consider successful learning? Have we assumed so much guilt about what the media tells us is the "poor" job schools are doing with students that we will literally dismantle the structure of our educational set-up in order to change things, to experiment with no certainty that results will be any better?

3 Are administrators remiss in not squelching overzealous teachers, notorious for their impracticality and tunnel vision? The administrators listen to and seem to concur with the teachers in the descriptions

above. Where is their leadership? Why don't the administrators provide guidelines for changes? Give teachers an inch, and you can't guarantee they won't ask for more modifications and "leeway."

4 Why can't teachers work within the current schedule to address their concerns about students' learning opportunities? Comment on teachers' efforts that you know of related to student advisory opportunities, enrichment and review in subject areas, research projects, and, of course, larger-than-they'd like English classes.

Comments

What justifies experimentation efforts such as those described in the case study? Shouldn't all changes result from exquisitely rigorous research studies? Some educational experts, on the other hand, advocate change for the sake of change. Isn't the reason for students' difficulty with courses and requirements the fact that they simply won't apply themselves and that we expect less and less of them? Note: *We* seem to change educational requirements all the time. Reform? It seems to be a mandate for ripping out the old structure and trying something— anything—new. Whole language learning, hands-on instruction, portfolios, projects, groups and teams, etc., testify to our willingness to try anything but the old-fashioned model, "teacher teaching and students learning." Where will it end? Will students learn more if we change everything?

PERFORMANCE OBJECTIVE

THE ADMINISTRATOR FACILITATES
PROCESSES AND ENGAGES IN
ACTIVITIES ENSURING THAT
—Emerging trends are recognized, studied,
  and applied as appropriate.

Case Study 56

As Mrs. Vela, the principal of Kaffie Elementary School, rounded the corner of the elementary wing, she heard loud voices that she recognized as those of Mrs. Allen, the third-grade teacher, and Mrs.

Prescott, her counterpart. When Mrs. Vela approached them, their voices were rising in a pitch that was not very professional. "Ladies, I realize this is after school, but what could be so important that you are almost yelling at each other?"

"Oh, Mrs. Vela, we were so involved in our discussion we did not hear you come up," said Mrs. Prescott, reddening slightly.

"We really were not yelling, Mrs. Vela," echoed Mrs. Allen. "We were just having a disagreement about the concept of whole language. She is for it and I am not."

Mrs. Prescott nodded her head vigorously. "I think we really need to adopt the concept of whole language in our district. Our students will benefit so much more by integrating all of the disciplines that we teach. Just last week, I used an old fairy tale. I was able to incorporate several science lessons and at least three math operations. My kids loved it."

"Oh, Marge," said Mrs. Allen in a chiding manner, "you are always ready to jump on any band wagon. I bet you would buy snake oil from a carnival barker if he told you it would improve your students' test scores."

"I am glad to see that you are both discussing professional issues even though your voices would indicate otherwise. I am here to ask you both to serve on the Textbook Committee. We will be examining the language arts components of English, spelling, reading, and handwriting. I am certain the matter of whole language and its usage will be addressed during these meetings, and you both can voice your active opinions."

Discussion Questions

1 How much involvement should a principal have in matters of curriculum?

2 How much involvement should a teacher have in matters of curriculum?

3 Do you feel that curriculum committees should consist of persons outside of education (e.g., parents or members of the site-based management team)?

4 When dealing with educational trends, how much research do you believe needs to be performed?

5 How do you tell the difference between a trend and a fad in education?

6 Should committees consist of persons as diametrically opposed as these two teachers?

7 As an administrator, how would you have handled this situation?

PERFORMANCE OBJECTIVE

THE ADMINISTRATOR FACILITATES
PROCESSES AND ENGAGES IN
ACTIVITIES ENSURING THAT
—Emerging trends are recognized, studied,
and applied as appropriate.

Case Study 57

A number of district teachers attended workshops, conferences, and national conventions last year, reporting back to colleagues about possible implications for the high school. Interested teacher committees formed at the end of the year to address specific concerns about students, related to the programs and policies of the high school. Committees reported and made recommendations at the first faculty meeting of the year. The groups represented findings on the issues listed below.

1 Sets of behavioral rules and expectations for students: Teachers discovered that many professionals attending special conference meetings had enjoyed improved classroom behavior by setting up rules, expectations, and consequences of infringements before they actually occurred. Students in each classroom joined with teachers to create the room rules, which would apply to all the entire year. Print shops created professional-looking signs in bold lettering to display in classrooms for all to see. Further, teachers sent copies of the rules home to all parent/guardians.

2 Course-content contracts for low-achieving students: Setting up contracts for completing all required assignments seemed to work well with chronically low-achieving students in subject-matter courses. These students were required to meet with their subject teachers, counselor, level advisor, assistant principal, and the dean throughout the academic year. The students received such positive feedback and encouragement that several dramatic turn-arounds resulted in one building. Parent/guardians were apprised of this before the first contract, and then teachers mailed copies of the contracts showing work completed to their homes. Phone calls resulted, with parents expressing gratitude. This technique required that the contract students were contacted by a group of committed, interested school personnel.

3 Alternative "school-within-a-school": Since some districts report problems with students who are substance abusers, many with chronic discipline and absence patterns, the school leaders sought special staff members to guide students in unique school settings. The creation of an alternative school, featuring caring but firm disciplinarians who would individualize programs for each student, in a single setting, was aided by external social service agencies and the student support services within the school. Parental/guardian input was required for all attendees. Progress was, admittedly, slow but effective, with an 80% retention rate for the year. Plans for this alternative are deemed realistic, given the possibility of students exhibiting these problems.

4 Conflict-resolution groups: The potential for violence in schools grows due to a variety of influences, to say nothing of violence routinely glorified in movies and on TV programs. Students respond well to "take time out to analyze and talk first" programs. The use of role-playing responses to critical incident vignettes brings students right into a conflict that needs resolution. Students learn how thinking through differences, avoiding confrontations, and not allowing minor skirmishes to escalate ultimately works to their advantage. Administrators and teachers reveal that students are impressed when they know how to employ an "alternative system" and save face when challenged by other students.

Discussion Questions

1 How do administrators, faculty, and staff learn about and assess current and emerging trends in order to make judgments about their appropriateness in specific school settings?

2 How do educational personnel know that a problem is, indeed, a problem that must be planned for and handled? This is meta-analysis, analyzing how we know a problem when we are confronted with one. It requires some thought. Is the fact that a single fight occurred on school property at the end of last year, for example, reason to jump on the "conflict-resolution" bandwagon?

3 What trends have been deemed significant enough to merit the attention of your school personnel? What steps have been taken to respond to these trends? What other trends that seem important in some school settings do not merit attention in your school?

4 Describe your responses to the four issues listed above: classroom behavior rules, contracts, alternative schools, and conflict resolution. Does each require careful adapting to each individual school?

5 Is it preferable to bring in outside help, specialists or consultants, to gain their objective viewpoints when evaluating emerging trends in education? Or is it crucial to utilize only the stakeholders in a given school community, the ones who may have firsthand knowledge of a problem or problems in the school?

6 Should a committee be created with the express purpose of researching educational publications and interviewing personnel in university programs who have knowledge of emerging trends in the field? Is it useful for this group to gather data reflecting national trends, per problem issue? Or should each department in the school react to their particular concerns, related to their subject matter?

7 Recommend three publications that could be used as sources for information on emerging trends in education. These might merit subscribing to and then collection in a professional "library" room for teachers and staff.

PERFORMANCE OBJECTIVE

THE ADMINISTRATOR FACILITATES
PROCESSES AND ENGAGES IN
ACTIVITIES ENSURING THAT
—Operational plans and procedures to
achieve the vision and goals of the school
are in place.

Case Study 58

When Hector Fuentes came to Blufftown as principal of the high school, he was amazed that the school had no mission statement or stated philosophy. In the two years since its completion, the school operated with no apparent goals or objectives. At his first teachers' meeting, he addressed his concerns with the faculty.

"I am concerned that we are all in a ship that has no rudder, and it certainly has no compass. You are all teaching in a vacuum. You have no concept of where you are ultimately going with the lessons you are teaching. I have never been in a district that did not have a mission statement or a philosophical statement already in place."

Several of the teachers shifted uncomfortably in their seats. "I propose that we form committees that will examine what we are doing as well as where we have been, and, most importantly, where we are headed. We must establish the means for our students to achieve our school's vision and goals. Make no mistake about it, we *need* a plan to follow, specific procedures to guide us as we strive to achieve our objectives, and a system of evaluation to track our progress in every course and program throughout this school."

A voice in the back of the auditorium was heard: "Mr. Fuentes, what do you really know about our school? We have been doing fine. We have managed to get along without you or your committees. Several of us feel these are just a waste of time. What will we have when we get finished besides a lot of time wasted and a lot of paper that no one will read?"

"I understand where you are coming from," answered Mr. Fuentes, "I know that what I am proposing is a lot of work. I do, however, disagree that it is a waste of time. We need a vision and we need goals. Without them, how do we know where we are going? Or, how do we know when we have arrived? As principal, I am going to require your participation in developing the mission statement and the goals and objectives for our school. I would rather do this than arbitrarily tell you what our mission will be."

Discussion Questions

1 How important is a schoolwide mission statement?
2 How important is a districtwide mission statement?

3 How much overlap can there be between the two mission statements?

4 Can a school operate without stated goals and objectives?

5 As a principal, how much input should you have into the mission statement?

6 As a principal, how much input should you have into the goals and objectives of the school?

7 How would you have reacted to the negative comment of the teacher in the back of the auditorium?

8 What input do you feel the staff should have in charting the course the school should be taking?

PERFORMANCE OBJECTIVE

THE ADMINISTRATOR FACILITATES
PROCESSES AND ENGAGES IN
ACTIVITIES ENSURING THAT
—Collective bargaining and other contractual
 agreements related to the school are
 effectively managed.

Case Study 59

After a long struggle, the contract between the school district and the teachers was finally approved by both sides and signed. As the administrators left the board meeting following final ratification, one of the principals commented to the superintendent, "I am sure glad this is over. We can forget about the contract for another year." The superintendent replied, "Actually, the contract is the first thing on tomorrow's administrative team agenda. See you there."

Discussion Questions

1 What could the superintendent mean? Why might it be on the agenda?

2 What things need to be done *after* the contract is signed?

Comments

It is important to make sure that all administrators in the school district know what changes have been made in the contract and why they have been made. For example, an item may have been added to the contract at the insistence of the teachers because of what happened in Maple School last year and the stance the administration took. To avoid a repeat, all administrators need to discuss this. It is helpful if the person who negotiated the contract for the board could meet with the administrators and go through the contract, item for item, telling them the changes, why they were made, what the teachers had said about each item, and how the administrators should administer the contract. Contract management is just as important as contract negotiations.

PERFORMANCE OBJECTIVE

THE ADMINISTRATOR FACILITATES
PROCESSES AND ENGAGES IN
ACTIVITIES ENSURING THAT
—Collective bargaining and other contractual
 agreements related to the school are
 effectively managed.

Case Study 60

One of the principals looked at the new teacher contract and asked to discuss the grievance procedure because there had never been any grievances in that building. "What do I do if someone comes in with a grievance?"

Discussion Questions

1 What advice should the superintendent give the principal?
2 What is the definition of a *grievance?* How does it differ from a teacher's complaint?
3 Does a principal have to give the teacher an answer immediately upon receiving the grievance? What advantages are there in waiting?

4 What should the principal do when the grievance arrives?

5 Sometimes several teachers in different buildings will turn in identical grievances in each building at the same time, hoping that the principals will give different responses to the same grievance. What can the district do to avoid such a situation?

Comments

All administrators who may be grieved should attend a meeting where these questions are discussed, after the new contract is approved and before any grievances are filed. A principal should be told that when a grievance is filed, no action should be taken or response given to the teacher. The principal should call the central office person responsible for negotiations (or maybe the superintendent in smaller districts), and tell them the grievance. By doing this, the district administration will know when anyone is filing a grievance. Also, the central office person can suggest wording for the grievance response (or even write it), knowing the contract well and knowing past practice and previous contract/grievance history.

PERFORMANCE OBJECTIVE

THE ADMINISTRATOR FACILITATES
PROCESSES AND ENGAGES IN
ACTIVITIES ENSURING THAT
—Collective bargaining and other contractual
agreements related to the school are
effectively managed.

Case Study 61

Because the negotiations had gone on so long, including a short teacher strike, the relationship between the board/administration and the teacher union was not very good. As the board members talked informally after the board meeting, following ratification, one member asked the superintendent what steps could be taken to improve the atmosphere.

Discussion Question

1 How would you, as superintendent, respond?

Comments

While each situation is different, here are some ideas that have worked for one of the authors:

- Administrators, including the superintendent, should spend time talking to teachers in the buildings.
- The superintendent could meet informally with the union president over breakfast or lunch, monthly, to discuss concerns that might become grievances if not addressed.
- The union leaders, superintendent, and board members might consider a dinner meeting to get to know each other away from the pressures of negotiations.
- The district could use the industry model of establishing a labor-management committee to meet on a regular basis to discuss problems.
- Following ratification, the superintendent and union president could issue a joint press release on the contract settlement, so that neither side will use the press to seek some public relations advantage right after negotiations are completed.

PERFORMANCE OBJECTIVE

THE ADMINISTRATOR FACILITATES
PROCESSES AND ENGAGES IN
ACTIVITIES ENSURING THAT
—The school plant, equipment, and support
  systems operate safely, efficiently, and
  effectively.

Case Study 62

One high school principal is almost overwhelmed in his first month on the job. He has a number of concerns, including:

- bus safety, bus drivers, bus maintenance (how to monitor necessary progress in these areas and field parent calls)
- maintenance tasks (three complaints surface: dirty locker and shower rooms; roaches in the downstairs bathrooms; less than clean, appealing classrooms, with accumulated dirt and dust everywhere, including floor cleaning residue in corners and along baseboards)
- cranky boiler that has required two repair calls already
- outdated, unsightly desks, classrooms, lab furniture and equipment
- cafeteria cooking facilities (cleanliness) and reports that boxed cheese has been seen loaded into cars after school hours

Discussion Questions

1 A new administrator needs good advice from experienced peers, especially if the assistant principal is unaware of some gritty realities or is so busy with pupil personnel tasks and monitoring day-by-day school problems that there is little time for discussion and problem-solving. Give the principal sound advice about each issue listed above.

2 Is it true that there are *always* complaints about the maintenance staff and outdated school furnishings in every school district except the wealthiest? Can a principal put these items ''on hold'' until less stressful times or when a break in the frantic daily pace occurs?

3 Is a ''Dr. Death Approach'' useful? That is, direct orders related to ''Do it now and do it my way'' can inspire results. Might it be appropriate to signal a change in administrators and styles of leadership, with more pointed directives to make changes and follow up, especially targeting changes not previously given attention to? What guidelines can you give to suggest how to soften the impact of changes in administrative style when a new member of the administrative team comes aboard? How can an administrator's style impact and facilitate necessary changes?

4 Is there any way for the principal to stay ahead of, anticipating and possibly derailing, problems in the listed areas? Is the use of time management strategies indicated? Explain.

Comments

A principal's understandable frustration can surface when the over-whelming challenges of overseeing building operations is a day-to-day reality. Obviously, one delegates authority, but still the problems command one's time and attention. Often, the day seems too short to get everything accomplished. How does one learn to prioritize daily problems? Unfortunately, university classes in effective school management may give short shrift to the daily, time-consuming problems that confront school leaders. A framework or model, a set of basic guide-lines, for operating successfully and efficiently may be necessary. Can you offer that framework or model, that set of basic guidelines?

PERFORMANCE OBJECTIVE

THE ADMINISTRATOR FACILITATES
PROCESSES AND ENGAGES IN
ACTIVITIES ENSURING THAT
—The school plant, equipment, and support
  systems operate safely, efficiently, and
  effectively.

Case Study 63

It was a cold Sunday afternoon in February when Dr. Kent arrived at Maplewood Middle School. All day he had been plagued with a nagging feeling that something was not right at the school. As he opened the door, a blast of hot, stagnant air hit him in the face. He sensed immediately that the temperature of the building was far above the 55 degree set-back that was used as an energy efficiency measure on weekends and during vacation time.

The office door handle was warm, almost hot, as he attempted to enter the office suite. Inside, Dr. Kent saw that the thermometer on the thermostat was a thin red line to the top of the glass. He reached for the telephone to call the head of maintenance. He received a busy signal. He then tried to call the assistant superintendent and found no one at home. He knew that his own custodial staff would not be in the building, since budgetary constraints had shortened their work week to five days instead of seven days.

Dr. Kent went to the boiler room. As he opened the door, he heard a loud thumping sound. When he turned on the light, he saw one of the three massive boilers literally bouncing several inches up and down. He fought the urge to turn and run from the building. Instead he looked in vain for some type of "kill switch" on the boiler. He found none. He looked at the clear sight glass and saw no water in the tube. "This is not a good sign," he mumbled aloud. It was then that he remembered a series of electrical boxes on the opposite wall. He ran to them and began to turn off the various switches and fuses. Finally, the boiler seemed to relax, and the thumping and bouncing began to subside.

The next morning, he met with the superintendent and the assistant superintendent involved in buildings and grounds operation and maintenance. "We found the problem with your boiler, Bob," said Mr. Menendez. "When the heating company changed a pump, they shut off the water to the boiler. They forgot to turn it on again. It is a lucky thing you happened to be in your building. Otherwise. . . ."

"I am glad I was there, too. But I know very little about the mechanical side of this school. I do, however, have a suggestion. I believe we need to install some type of a 'kill switch' so the boiler can be shut down quickly should an emergency arise. I also want teachers in the vicinity of the boiler room to have an understanding of emergency shut-down procedures should we ever need to use them."

Discussion Questions

1 Should principals be required to be school managers, who understand the mechanical side of equipment and support systems?

2 Should Dr. Kent have called the maintenance staff first, or should he have attempted to remedy the problem himself?

3 Could there be a better way to handle emergency situations such as this?

4 What emergency procedures would you implement in your school to prevent hazardous situations?

5 Do you think Dr. Kent's idea of involving teachers is professionally sound?

PERFORMANCE OBJECTIVE

THE ADMINISTRATOR FACILITATES
PROCESSES AND ENGAGES IN
ACTIVITIES ENSURING THAT
—Time is managed to maximize attainment
of organizational goals.

Case Study 64

"We are sick and tired of being treated like second-class citizens, Mike," said Mr. Vernon as he glared across the desk at Mike London, the principal. Mr. Vernon, the long-time union president, was in a foul mood after receiving several complaints from his membership about extra time involving staff development. "You and your superintendent cannot, and should not, arbitrarily demand that the teachers of this district attend workshops after they have put in an entire day teaching."

"What do you propose we do, Sam?" asked the principal. "You know as well as I do that staff development is an important component to keep our teachers on the cutting edge. When do you propose we do it?"

"I do agree that staff development is important. I do not agree that it be scheduled in an arbitrary manner. Besides, how can you expect teachers to concentrate when they are completely worn out? Eight hours in a classroom and then three more in a meeting is more than anyone should be expected to spend."

At that point, Mrs. Stilwell, the superintendent, entered the principal's office. "I am sorry I am late," she expressed as she hurriedly took her seat. Both men quickly explained what had been discussed in her absence.

Mrs. Stilwell looked at Mike and then at Sam. "I think Sam has an excellent point. Maybe we have been too hasty in our attempt to initiate our professional staff development program. Perhaps we need to poll the teachers to find out what they need to assist them in their professional goals. As to Sam's concern about a long work day, I agree. I, for one, do not like to work as long as I do. I am certain you do not either, Mike."

"Sam, I am not going to give you a firm answer at this time about the 'when'; I am, however, going to examine the budget to see if we can afford some half-days and if we can bring in some substitute teachers to free up our teaching staff. If we use substitutes, our staff members are more likely to be receptive to the inservice efforts we feel are so necessary. We can try it for our next scheduled staff development workshop.''

Discussion Questions

1 As an administrator, how would you cope with planning staff development?

2 How much input do you feel teachers should be allowed? What structure should be established to formulate staff development programs?

3 We all agree that staff development is important. How would you react to the budget side of this process?

4 How do you think the public will react to teachers doing staff development during the teaching day while using substitute teachers at the taxpayers' expense?

5 Do you think the superintendent was wise in her dealings with the union president?

6 As a principal, how would you have reacted in this situation? to the superintendent's comments?

7 How do you weigh the importance of student time-on-task and time for teacher staff development?

8 Could there be some compromise, such as starting the program before the usual school dismissal time and staying after that time, too?

PERFORMANCE OBJECTIVE

THE ADMINISTRATOR FACILITATES
PROCESSES AND ENGAGES IN
ACTIVITIES ENSURING THAT
—Potential problems and opportunities are
  identified.

Case Study 65

Calk Elementary School was an imposing two-story brick edifice—built in the 1930s, sitting on a hill in the middle of a quiet residential neighborhood. Mrs. Daniels, the principal, knew that the building needed refurbishing and modernizing, but until little Danny Gomez and his parents came to town, she did not realize what problems Calk had. Danny Gomez, a second grader, was a paraplegic confined to a wheelchair. His parents, Arturo and Eida, expressed immediate concern and displeasure that the facility was not equipped for handicapped students. "Haven't you people heard of the Americans with Disabilities Act?" Mr. Gomez asked the principal.

"Of course, we have, Mr. and Mrs. Gomez. We are cognizant of the Act and its implications for the district in general and Calk Elementary in particular. You do have to understand, however, that Calk was built 60 years before the inception of the ADA. I want to assure you that we will do everything in our power to make Danny's time in our school a pleasant and rewarding experience."

"I am sure you will," said Mrs. Gomez. "Danny is our only son, and we are concerned about his welfare. How do you propose to deal with Danny's handicap?"

"I intend to have the district's maintenance crew install ramps for Danny. I will also request that we provide handicapped restroom facilities for his use. I will check with the plumbers, and we will also provide a drinking fountain that is wheelchair accessible. If Danny needs any other accommodations, please do not hesitate to let me know."

"I do have a question for you, Mrs. Daniels. What is going to happen when Danny has to go to the second floor?" asked Mr. Gomez. "Will you provide an elevator for him?"

"I think," answered an astounded Mrs. Daniels, "that an elevator may be out of the question. Calk is not designed for an elevator, nor do we have a budget that could withstand the installation of an elevator. My suggestion is that we schedule all of Danny's classes on the first floor. Our upper grades are on the second floor, but by the time Danny is ready to be in those grades, we will simply move the teacher and the class to the first floor for that particular year."

Mr. Gomez turned to his wife and said, "I think Danny will be happy here. Thank you, Mrs. Daniels, for being sensitive to our son's needs."

Discussion Questions

1 Should school districts be forced to comply with the Americans with Disabilities Act?

2 Should school districts be forced to renovate or even close buildings that do not comply with federal laws like the ADA?

3 Do you feel that Mr. and Mrs. Gomez were realistic in expecting an elevator to be installed in Calk Elementary School?

4 Do you feel that Mrs. Daniels acted in an appropriate manner in her dealings with Danny's handicap?

5 If you were the principal, would you have involved members of the teaching staff in your decisions?

6 How would you handle a situation like this if you were Mrs. Daniels? if you were Mr. and Mrs. Gomez?

PERFORMANCE OBJECTIVE

THE ADMINISTRATOR FACILITATES
PROCESSES AND ENGAGES IN
ACTIVITIES ENSURING THAT
—Problems are confronted and resolved in a
  timely manner.

Case Study 66

Derrick Arredondo was called into assistant principal Ketcham's office. "Derrick, I am afraid we are going to have to expel you from school for fighting in the cafeteria today. You are out of here until further notice." According to the state legal code, Mr. Ketcham should have contacted Derrick's mother within 24 hours of Derrick's removal. Unfortunately, other school matters intervened and Mr. Ketcham did not remember Derrick's dismissal until the following week.

"Mr. Ketcham, I received a telephone call from a Mrs. Arredondo inquiring why her son was expelled. Do you know anything about this? I certainly did not!"

"Oh my gosh, Mike!" Mr. Ketcham said to Mike Taft, the principal of Beachside High School. "I completely forgot to do the follow-up.

It has been several days, and I know we are supposed to inform the parent within 24 hours. I am sorry. I simply got busy and forgot.''

"You really dropped the ball on this one, Kevin," said the principal. "This lady has a real case against your decision. You did not inform her, and you did not have a hearing before you expelled him. You basically violated state law and the rights of the student. I know you are new to the position of assistant principal, but you have to follow the law and school district procedures.''

"Again, I am sorry. Is there anything that we can do to salvage this situation? I mean, Derrick was in a fight in the cafeteria. He struck a boy who was identified as a special education student.''

"I think," said the principal, "that we had better get Mrs. Arredondo and her son in here as soon as possible. I agree there has to be a punishment, but I am concerned about the legality of the situation. We need to be certain that Derrick does not think that he can get off with a slap on the wrist, but we cannot enforce the expulsion because of your failure to follow procedure. I think I can convince Mrs. Arredondo that her son needs to be punished, but we will do it without using the expulsion as the punishment.''

"I appreciate your backing me on a punishment, Mr. Taft. Derrick does need disciplinary action. I know his mother, and I believe she will agree with our decision. I will get them in as quickly as possible.''

"In the future, Kevin, please be certain that you follow procedural requirements.''

Discussion Questions

1 Do you feel that an assistant principal should be allowed to expel a student without consulting the principal?

2 Do you feel that an assistant principal should have legal and procedural training immediately upon receiving the position?

3 Was Mr. Ketcham correct in telling Derrick that he was expelled, or should he have used different terminology?

4 What would your reaction be to Mrs. Arredondo's call if you were the principal, Mr. Taft?

5 Do you believe that Mr. Taft handled the situation with Mr. Ketcham in an appropriate manner?

6 Do you believe that Mr. Taft handled the situation with Derrick and his mother in an appropriate manner?

7 Do you believe that Mrs. Arredondo could have successfully challenged Mr. Ketcham's decision to expel her son?

8 In your state, what is the definition of a *suspension* and an *expulsion*? What is the difference? Who can suspend or expel, and for how long? What are the procedures required by state law? by your own district?

PERFORMANCE OBJECTIVE

THE ADMINISTRATOR FACILITATES
PROCESSES AND ENGAGES IN
ACTIVITIES ENSURING THAT
—Financial, human, and material resources
  are aligned to the goals of schools.

Case Study 67

"My son is going to be in the sixth grade this year," said Mrs. Snyder, a second-term board member, to Ralph Hawkins, the principal of Woodville Middle School. "I personally think you have too many students in your classes. I want you to hire some additional teachers so that the students will receive more additional attention."

Hawkins knew when Mrs. Snyder came into his office unannounced that he would have difficulties with her. As a board member, her interest lay in whatever areas affected her son. Hawkins knew that for the past several years the elementary teachers and the elementary principal had had to deal with her demands and her personal agenda. Mr. Hawkins knew that he had to make a stand. "Mrs. Snyder," he began, "I really appreciate your taking the time to come and see me. I know you are concerned for your son, and I want to take this opportunity to calm any fears that you may be experiencing. You and the other board members approve our district budget. As you well know, the board asks for each of the principals' inputs and requests. From that, we try to build the most functional budget we can. I want to assure you that our middle school has an acceptable, and I think some would say *enviable,* teacher-to-student ratio. All of our curricular offerings follow a middle school format and adhere to state mandates. Our middle school has been developed by design and not by happenstance, Mrs. Snyder. You, above all people, should understand our district's mission statement as well as our budgetary constraints. I simply cannot comply with your request to add staff in an arbitrary manner. We have our goals. We have our objectives. We also have our staff in place as dictated by these specifications. And we have our budget in place. We are operating on a given course. I believe we are successfully achieving our stated objectives. Forgive me for saying this, Mrs. Snyder, but you are just one person. I do not think you are speaking for the entire board. If the board and the superintendent direct me to hire additional teachers, I will do so. Until then, I think we have a sufficient program. If you allow us, we will try to make your son's time with us worthwhile.''

Discussion Questions

1 Do you agree with the principal's stand regarding arbitrary hiring of additional teachers?

2 How would you deal with a parent/board member like Mrs. Snyder?

3 Do you think the principal handled the situation in an appropriate manner?

4 How important is a mission statement to the overall performance of a particular school?

5 What is the unique difference between a board member's directive and a board's directive?

6 Did Mrs. Snyder direct her concerns to the appropriate administrator?

7 Did Mrs. Snyder's concern have any validity?

8 Even if a board member's demands are not "board action," are there consequences for not following them? Should a board member be treated like any other parent?

PERFORMANCE OBJECTIVE

THE ADMINISTRATOR FACILITATES
PROCESSES AND ENGAGES IN
ACTIVITIES ENSURING THAT
—Financial, human, and material resources
  are aligned to the goals of the schools.

Case Study 68

The administrative team members talk about a variety of resources for the school and students, utilized and underutilized, that are aligned with their goals. In this school, the goals include academic achievement and mastery of basics for all students and students' recognition of their abilities and interests, specifically related to future education, jobs, and careers.

Team members review *financial* resources heretofore untapped. They understand that five national and global corporations in their state are looking to underwrite "good causes" and, perhaps, sponsor new efforts in school districts. This team concurs that there are desired activities that need funding from outside school: an art fair to feature student work in all media, a band competition on the East coast (new uniforms are really necessary, too), and the concert band's invitation to perform with the city orchestra in a special concert.

The administrators also turn to *human* resources. They feel they have neglected to fully utilize the local chapters of the DAR and the League of Women Voters; social service agency personnel; Kiwanis club members and their scholarships; representatives of two industries locally, a chemical company and a manufacturer of eyeglass frames; university placement services for information related to job sources and job trends; Internet connections with universities countrywide; and tutors, the Retired Teachers Corps.

However, *material* resources are also necessary. Students need to access special computer programs related to exploring their career interests, if not to explore their abilities, talents, and skills with the intent of identifying possible jobs and careers. The administrators cite exploration of computer available enrichment programs. One team member, aware that research projects and term papers are a necessity for many students in the school, wonders why it would not be possible to get groups of students into the local community college and/or university library, say, perhaps, on a supervised "field trip." Distance learning opportunities may also be available; where does one locate a list of programs available? Chances are good that a review of "Modern Jazz Masters" or the five-part "Overview of American History," advertised in a student-oriented "bulletin" on-line, could benefit students.

Discussion Questions

1 Describe your impressions about the usefulness of the financial, human and material resources cited above.

2 What financial, human, and material resources do many schools overlook? Comment on those resources sought for your school's students and the effects of utilizing them. Review, for example, various departments that utilize extra resources.

3 If stakeholders value additional resources for students, what means can be used to list and, ultimately, pursue these? Is there a point at which resources detract from efforts to teach the school's basic course of study? What guidelines might you offer administrators regarding the latter point?

4 Is a needs assessment and priority list of available resources a help or a hindrance?

Comments

Schools, in many cases, lack funds and the resources to supplement existing educational programs. In addition, there is a variety of supplemental services and offerings useful for students in almost all communities. Fortunately, reform efforts have opened school doors to input from "outsiders"; often, mutual benefits accrue. A changing school population may utilize resources undreamed of in previous eras, such as corporate sponsorships, company internship programs, and guest speakers who share perspectives about the working world. The limit to seeking and using resources beyond those provided by the school may, ultimately, be student needs. Dedication to academic achievement for all students and their recognition of abilities keyed to future education, jobs, and careers may require seeking supplemental resources to meet their varied needs.

PERFORMANCE OBJECTIVE

THE ADMINISTRATOR FACILITATES
PROCESSES AND ENGAGES IN
ACTIVITIES ENSURING THAT
—The school acts entrepreneurally to support
  continuous improvement.

Case Study 69

"Ladies and gentlemen," superintendent Louis Ellis addressed his principals, "the state has once again seen fit to level-fund us. As most of you know, the state has done this for the past six years, and we have worn out our welcome with the local finance board. Our community simply does not have the tax base required to support our educational needs. I am open for suggestions."

Milton Kelly, the elder statesman among the principals, looked at the budget figures in front of him and laughed. "Lou," he said, "we have got to stop taking this lying down. I think we need to become more aggressive."

"Not with our local politicians, Milt. After all, you cannot get blood from an apple."

"My mother used to say *turnip,* Lou. And, I was not referring to local property taxes. I was thinking more along the lines of colleges and universities. You know, partnerships, endowments, and the like."

"That's great for you, Milt," said Mary Dunbar, one of the elementary principals. "You and your high school will hog all of the glory and, if I know you, all of the money."

"I am deeply hurt, Mary," said Milt with a grin.

"Mary is probably right, Milt," said the superintendent. "But let's talk about it."

Milt's face took on a serious look as he leaned forward in his chair. "I envision us—the entire district—embarking upon a sales campaign to local and surrounding businesses and industries. They could sponsor Adopt-a-School programs, provide speakers and field trips, and even lend expertise in various subject areas. I especially see them sponsoring special projects and programs."

Mary looked enthusiastic as she continued to build upon Milt's ideas: "I see various businesses and industries providing us with computers that may be obsolete for them but that we could put to good use. I even see some of these places providing equipment that could be used in our science classrooms."

"I like the way you two are thinking," said the superintendent. "I think this may be an excellent way to supplement our flagging budget and to advertise our critical needs to people of importance."

Discussion Questions

1 How much are budgets affected by the current political climate?

2 Is it a good idea for principals and even superintendents to solicit help?

3 Discuss the positives of this type of plan as well as the negatives.

4 How would you initiate a program like this to ensure its success?

5 Is there a danger in having people think that this program will solve the financial problems, or is it more likely that it will bring the problems to light?

6 Are you aware of schools with successful foundation programs? with successful partnerships with businesses?

7 If partnerships are extended to businesses, what can principals offer to the businesses?

PERFORMANCE OBJECTIVE

THE ADMINISTRATOR FACILITATES
PROCESSES AND ENGAGES IN
ACTIVITIES ENSURING THAT
—The school acts entrepreneurally to support
  continuous improvement.

Case Study 70

"I think we could all use a few lessons from business," begins the principal at the faculty meeting. "Oh, I know the education–business comparison is not as exact as some theorists would have us believe, but let's take a look at some key practices and strategies that businesses take very seriously and see if those relate to our purposes." The principal specifies some important features, as listed.

- business plan and goals: The school district is strongly committed to its vision of learning for students, as well as the carefully constructed goals and objectives. The principal encourages all faculty to work within the guidelines provided by the vision, goals, and objectives, and she wants to know about implementation efforts of all teachers. She further challenges them to suggest revisions and improvements deemed necessary.

- accountability: In addition to feedback that will occur when state and national assessment tests are given, the principal cites the "rather informal" systems of evaluation the district has used in reviewing professional evaluations. She explains an alternative, Management by Objectives, which all members of the professional staff, administrators, faculty, and noncertificated staff will soon become much more familiar with.
- job descriptions: The principal asks for input to create job descriptions for all noncertificated staff in the building. She has created a document that allows those not involved in those jobs to specify the most needed tasks of key personnel in the building. She reveals that the noncertificated personnel will evolve their own job descriptions and that all documents per position will be carefully scanned, content discussed, and that final descriptions created.
- marketing/advertising strategy: Here the principal targets one of her favorite subjects, effective communication efforts between schools and community, between schools and the homes of all students. "Let's also get some good school news out there via local media!" She will use a consultant to conduct a workshop on telephone techniques, effective written documents, and, especially, the *tone* of all messages, to remind everyone about the need for establishing and maintaining favorable impressions.
- competition analysis: "Other schools have reinstated some interesting mini-courses, new options and other electives for students," she begins. "District 201 has a project physics class and a mathematics course for potential engineers. I want to investigate our revising and/or creating new courses to challenge and interest students. They worked well before; we can make them work again. Please sign up for committee assignments on this vital topic."
- improved product: The principal targets another area of interest, improvement of instruction and investigation of new methods to engage students at all levels of learning. She suggests that all departments study the availability of pertinent university courses

and attendance at relevant workshops, conferences, and conventions. She wants those ideas brought back for discussion and implementation in the school, if applicable.

Discussion Questions

1 Is the education–business analogy taken too seriously? What, specifically, can those involved in education learn from the hustlers in businesses?

2 The principal has not alluded to several other key business priorities, including (1) a supplies, equipment, and needs list, (2) the geographic market area, (3) the executive summary, (4) knowing the customer and the customer base, (5) the site location, and (6) business risk. Comment on how relevant or important any or all of these six are, as they apply to schools and education.

3 If the principal is so interested in business applications, might she invite local entrepreneurs to a series of meetings with her administrative team? Discussion could center on business efforts with work teams, multicultural work settings, downsizing, restructuring/reengineered companies, and the use of contract workers and consultants. The entrepreneurs' input about how to prepare students for the workplace and their expectations of new employees might be enlightening. They might also offer valuable perspectives about economic trends, regionally, nationally, and globally.

4 Give the principal your perspective about empowering parent and community committees to study programs and policies, extracurricular offerings, and a series of suggestions for improving all phases of education in the school. Their involvement is vital, yet few volunteer to take the time necessary to study issues and make recommendations.

5 Are such documents as an annual report or a school's report card necessary to a school's improvement efforts? Review and comment on your experience with these documents and their success or lack of it.

6 Offer your perspective about other business "connections" that you know are vital to schools' efforts, including business theories and practices, as well as "borrowing" standard business operating

procedures. Think in terms of enhancing the organization, operations, and resources of a school and its providing a safe, efficient, and effective learning situation for students.

PERFORMANCE OBJECTIVE

THE ADMINISTRATOR FACILITATES
PROCESSES AND ENGAGES IN
ACTIVITIES ENSURING THAT
—Organizational systems are regularly
monitored and modified as needed.

Case Study 71

Mrs. Peterson, principal of Brown Middle School, called her staff together on a warm afternoon in late spring. "I have just returned from three series of meetings at the administration building," she said to the teachers. "We have decided that we need to be more accessible and flexible in our school district. To this end, we are now going to initiate a site-based, decision-making team concept."

"Just exactly what is that, Mrs. Peterson?" asked Connie Thompson, the home economics teacher. "I do not remember hearing that term in my education classes."

"That is because dinosaurs had not been invented when you were in college," said Mr. Holcomb, the language arts teacher and comedian-in-residence.

"I am glad you asked that, Connie," answered the principal, ignoring Mr. Holcomb's comment. "A site-based management team is a group of people—teachers, administrators, community members and parents—who help guide and direct what is occurring in particular schools in the district."

"Is this another committee you will be in charge of?" asked Celina Brown, the librarian.

"No, Mrs. Brown. I will not be running the site-based meetings. I will be there, but only in an advisory capacity. It will be you, the teachers, and the community members who will help us chart the goals and objectives that need to be achieved. It is my understanding that this will be done through consensus building.''

''If what you say is true, that would certainly put a lot of pressure on the staff,'' interjected Mrs. Thompson.

''No, I really do not see it that way,'' said the principal. ''I see it as an opportunity for you as teachers to have genuine input in how your school is operated. I really think you will be able to demonstrate your leadership potential. After all, I feel we are blessed with teachers who are true professionals.''

''Now let me get this straight,'' said Mr. Holcomb. ''If we are members of the site-based decision-making team, we actually get to make decisions about issues that affect each of us and our students?''

''That is what the lady said, John,'' interjected Mrs. Thompson. ''We are finally getting a chance to do something that will benefit everyone. Why don't you listen instead of talking for a change?''

''I realize it is late, and I can see that several of you have had a long and hard day, so I just want to close by thanking you for listening and for your input. I really and truly believe that site-based decision-making will be of great benefit to our school, and it is one more way to express our professionalism. I also want to assure you that if something is decided upon by the committee and later proves to be inappropriate or unworkable, it can certainly be reexamined. I see this as a win-win situation for us all.''

Discussion Questions

1 What is your understanding of a site-based decision-making team?
2 Should the administration have asked for more input from the teachers before deciding to implement site-based decision-making?
3 How effective do you think this top-down approach will be?
4 Would you have handled the implementation at your school in the same way or in a different manner than Mrs. Peterson?
5 What type of relationship do you feel the principal had with the staff?
6 Are Mrs. Peterson's expectations too ambitious for this staff?
7 How would you go about establishing a site-based decision-making team at your school?

8 What would be the role of the principal in this team?

9 Would all school faculties receive this news in the same way?

10 What type of principal would work best under this system?

11 Should the principal be obligated to implement all decisions, even if she disagreed? What if the faculty, as a whole, seemed to disagree with a decision of the committee? Are there appeal processes that could be built into the system for the principal and for the faculty when they felt a decision was wrong?

PERFORMANCE OBJECTIVE

THE ADMINISTRATOR FACILITATES
PROCESSES AND ENGAGES IN
ACTIVITIES ENSURING THAT
—Organizational systems are regularly
  monitored and modified as needed.

Case Study 72

Note these organizational systems common to most schools:

- the communication network (routine and emergency messages)
- the school's sports program
- the board of education, its policy decisions
- the buildings and grounds (maintenance) network
- the top-down hierarchy: administrators, teachers, support staff

Discussion Question

1 Describe how each of the above organizational systems can be regularly monitored and modified as needed. Suggest guidelines for administrators to follow, providing specific examples as needed based upon your own knowledge and experience. As you formulate responses, consider that the ultimate goal is a safe, efficient, and effective learning environment.

Comments

A school's communication network is vital, especially when hazardous weather conditions prevail or when unexpected emergencies arise (plumbing problems, gas leakages, paint fumes). An example addresses the importance of a monitored, effective, workable organizational system.

One school relies on the superintendent who calls a radio station and a local television station to report the school's closing. But the superintendent waits until the latest possible moment (usually at 8:00 A.M., the time scheduled for the start of the first class period) to announce the school's infrequent closings. It is a matter of personal pride for this administrator to keep the school open, no matter what.

The superintendent closed the school recently in the midst of an ice storm that had started well after midnight. Streets were sheets of thick ice. Unfortunately, as usually occurs with the closing of the high school, some faculty and staff members who live some distance away started out very early and had already arrived at school when the announcement was made. They had entered the building and were in their rooms, expecting business as usual. In addition, some parents, concerned about their children's safety and fully aware of media reports (one reporter said, simply, while reading a list of over 50 school closings in the viewing area, ''Believe it or not, we haven't—repeat have *not*—received word from Southern High School as yet''), had driven their children to school and were irate to learn the school had closed for the day. Can the personal pride of an administrator sometimes get in the way of common sense?

PERFORMANCE OBJECTIVE

THE ADMINISTRATOR FACILITATES
PROCESSES AND ENGAGES IN
ACTIVITIES ENSURING THAT

—Stakeholders are involved in decisions
  affecting schools.

Case Study 73

Aware that parental involvement is crucial to students' success, J. Principal decides that this is going to be Parental Involvement Year in District 203. J. considers the following a start:

- Create 10:00 A.M. "coffee break" information/dialogue sessions open to anyone interested in attending (to be held monthly in principal's conference room); invite local newspaper people.
- Suggest that the board devote a portion of each monthly meeting to "sensitive issue" curricular and course offerings (novels and nonfiction read in English classes, the "safe sex" unit in health education class, an exhaustive Holocaust unit, the gay/lesbian perspective and AIDS awareness from Issues in Contemporary Science class, etc.). Teachers would present their views and explain courses and units, but listen for concerns of parent/guardians and community members.
- Contact each parent/guardian with a personal invitation to attend Back to School Night and Open House activities. Create a folder for each attendee at the events, publish a program with maps, teachers' names, student schedule, administrator locations.
- Write a column in the local newspaper (and feature some of the ideas in the district newsletter) about the impact parents have on students' education, using parental/guardian interviews, quotations from students, selected suggestions from research studies, and the opinions of leading psychologists.
- Invite local social service agencies to deliver presentations every month (Concern for Youth series) about salient issues: discipline in the home; dealing with peer pressure; motivating children; keeping children drug-free, alcohol-free; signs of troubled youth, depression and suicide indicators; child and adolescent developmental stages; preparation for careers and college: when to start, how to start; freedom vs. responsibility: too much or too little? and gang information.
- Participate in the PTA evening "dessert" sessions held in various PTA members' homes throughout the year; this is a relaxed, open forum to receive and respond to a variety of parental/guardian concerns.

- Encourage coaches of all sports to hold special introductory meetings with parent/guardians before the start of each season. Distribute and discuss the District 203 Athletics Code of Conduct and the philosophy of the district; coaches will represent the views of the administration at this meeting.
- Start a HOTLINE: School Issues information phone service allowing parent/guardians to speak to a professional in the social service agencies in town, with advisory for local district administrators, as necessary.
- Invite any parent/guardians interested to attend the Policy Committee meetings (all issues related to School District 203, with membership from administrators, teachers, students, community people, parent/guardians), to be held on a rotating timetable to accommodate a variety of schedules. Publish list of topics covered last year (athletic eligibility, portfolio assessment, senior trip, junior high Washington trip, Homecoming festivities, tardy policy).

Discussion Questions

1 How can the principal ensure parent/guardian participation in each of these opportunities? Has the principal covered all the bases?
2 Is a survey necessary first to determine what topics interest parents?
3 What other opportunities may appeal to parent/guardians? Relate your experience to topics that include academics, sports, extracurricular opportunities, regional and social issues.
4 How has your district responded to the challenge of involving parent/guardians in young people's education?

Comments

Eliciting parent/guardian feedback means being sensitive to their job schedules and free times. You might need to have meetings taped and shown on local television stations. Allow "open phone line" times where those interested can call in and discuss a variety of concerns. Making the school more a community resource than a forbidding bureaucracy also helps. In addition, faculty and staff participation in community organizations should be encouraged so that people in the community get to know school people outside the school setting.

PERFORMANCE OBJECTIVE

THE ADMINISTRATOR FACILITATES
PROCESSES AND ENGAGES IN
ACTIVITIES ENSURING THAT
—Responsibility is shared to maximize
ownership and accountability.

Case Study 74

Jim Johnson, the high school principal, was going through his agenda with the Principal's Advisory Committee. He had told the teachers that he had established procedures for the annual open house and had explained them in detail. Then he talked about new disciplinary rules that he had established and the procedures that teachers should follow. The next item on the agenda was "textbooks." He told the committee that he had spent many hours going through the various junior English anthologies, paperbacks, etc., before arriving at a decision. Finally, he explained in detail how he had determined what supplies to order for the next semester. He was somewhat surprised that no one had any questions as the committee members quietly left the room.

Discussion Questions

1 What's wrong with this picture?
2 What did Mr. Johnson probably think was the function of this committee?
3 When elected to this committee, what might the new members think was the function of the committee?
4 If you see a difference in the responses in #2 and #3, what problems does that cause?
5 In each example from the agenda, how could committee members or other faculty members become involved?

6 Does it really make a difference if teachers take ownership in something by working on it? What are some examples where teachers were really involved in decision-making and, as a result of this ownership, the project was a success?

7 Sometimes administrators say that teachers are willing to participate in the decisions as long as they are not held responsible for the result. Is this sometimes true? From each standpoint (principal, teacher), is this satisfactory?

8 There are different types of decisions. Some advisory committees are asked to make decisions like picking the date and time of the open house and deciding what refreshments to serve. Other committees (or groups of teachers) are asked to help interview new teacher candidates or help re-write the school disciplinary procedures. Do you see the difference between these two types of decisions? How will teachers react if they always are asked to make the first type of decisions? the second type?

9 Discuss the following statement: When you share decision-making with others, you do not lose power as an administrator; you actually increase your power.

PERFORMANCE OBJECTIVES

THE ADMINISTRATOR FACILITATES
PROCESSES AND ENGAGES IN
ACTIVITIES ENSURING THAT
—Effective problem-framing and problem-
  solving skills are used.
—Effective group-process and consensus-
  building skills are used.

Three techniques that are often used for group decision-making are the following:

1 Interacting Group Technique—The leader explains a situation or problem and asks the group to discuss it. After discussion, the leader asks the group to arrive at a consensus or to vote on a solution.

2 Nominal Group Technique—The leader explains a situation and asks the group to write down solutions individually with no discussion. Then group members write their solutions on a chalkboard or paper or tell them to the group, again without any discussion or comments. When all solutions have been written, discussion occurs. Then, the group has a silent vote on the final solution.

3 Delphi Group Technique—This is used when the group cannot be assembled in one place. The leader usually writes to the group members and asks them to rank order whatever list is under consideration. The leader tabulates the results and sends the list out again to the same people, telling them the results of the ranking. The group members rank the items again. The results are tabulated. Sometimes this process is done a third time to obtain the final ranking of the group.

Directions: For each case study listed (Case Studies 75–80), decide which of the three techniques would be appropriate, tell why you chose it, and explain how it would be used in the case study.

Case Study 75

The principal wants his faculty to make a decision about whether to hold an open house as has been done in the past or take a different approach to welcoming parents into the school.

Discussion Questions

1 Which of the three techniques mentioned prior to Case Study 75 would be appropriate for this case study?

2 Why would you choose this technique?

3 How would the technique be used in this case study?

PERFORMANCE OBJECTIVES

THE ADMINISTRATOR FACILITATES
PROCESSES AND ENGAGES IN
ACTIVITIES ENSURING THAT
—Effective problem-framing and problem-
solving skills are used.
—Effective group-process and consensus-
building skills are used.

Case Study 76

The principal wants her faculty to make a decision about whether to have the inservice day handled by the faculty themselves or invite outside speakers to the school to talk about a topic.

Discussion Questions

1 Which of the three techniques mentioned prior to Case Study 75 would be appropriate for this case study?
2 Why would you choose this technique?
3 How would the technique be used in this case study?

PERFORMANCE OBJECTIVES

THE ADMINISTRATOR FACILITATES
PROCESSES AND ENGAGES IN
ACTIVITIES ENSURING THAT
—Effective problem-framing and problem-
   solving skills are used.
—Effective group-process and consensus-
   building skills are used.

Case Study 77

The principal wants to sample graduates of the high school and have them choose the top five or six outstanding features of the high school. They will also single out which areas need improvement.

Discussion Questions

1 Which of the three techniques mentioned prior to Case Study 75 would be appropriate for this case study?
2 Why would you choose this technique?
3 How would the technique be used in this case study?

PERFORMANCE OBJECTIVES

THE ADMINISTRATOR FACILITATES
PROCESSES AND ENGAGES IN
ACTIVITIES ENSURING THAT
—Effective problem-framing and problem-
solving skills are used.
—Effective group-process and consensus-
building skills are used.

Case Study 78

The principal wants the faculty to make a decision about whether
to eliminate elementary music and elementary art, or suggest some
way to save these areas without spending the amount currently required.
This issue has been a source of controversy in the district.

Discussion Questions

1 Which of the three techniques mentioned prior to Case Study 75
would be appropriate for this case study?
2 Why would you choose this technique?
3 How would the technique be used in this case study?

PERFORMANCE OBJECTIVE

THE ADMINISTRATOR FACILITATES
PROCESSES AND ENGAGES IN
ACTIVITIES ENSURING THAT
—Effective problem-framing and problem-
solving skills are used.
—Effective group-process and consensus-
building skills are used.

Case Study 79

A teacher with a strong personality plans to present a problem (and
his solution) to the faculty. The principal wants the faculty to make a

decision, but he does not want them to agree to the man's solution just because of his forcefulness.

Discussion Questions

1 Which of the three techniques mentioned prior to Case Study 75 would be appropriate for this case study?
2 Why would you choose this technique?
3 How would the technique be used in this case study?

PERFORMANCE OBJECTIVES

THE ADMINISTRATOR FACILITATES
PROCESSES AND ENGAGES IN
ACTIVITIES ENSURING THAT
—Effective problem-framing and problem-
   solving skills are used.
—Effective group-process and consensus-
   building skills are used.

Case Study 80

In July, the principal wants to establish goals for the next year by seeking the opinions of his teachers, many parents, and some community members.

Discussion Questions

1 Which of the three techniques mentioned prior to Case Study 75 would be appropriate for this case study?
2 Why would you choose this technique?
3 How would the technique be used in this case study?

PERFORMANCE OBJECTIVE

THE ADMINISTRATOR FACILITATES
PROCESSES AND ENGAGES IN
ACTIVITIES ENSURING THAT
—Effective conflict-resolution skills are used.

Case Study 81

A number of conflicts are to be expected in most school settings, as is the case in almost all work situations. Note the examples of professionals who have conflicts in one school district:

- fervent unionizers versus teachers who dislike and oppose teachers' unions
- department members versus department members (same or "competing" departments)
- the new curriculum director versus almost every single teacher in the school
- the superintendent versus the board
- the superintendent versus teachers

Discussion Questions

1 Some might argue that all professional members of the school community are united in a single effort to deliver educational services to students and that this is each professional's priority. Yet, philosophies differ and the means to the goal are often as unique as those who subscribe to them. Disputes and conflicts are inevitable. Many experts blame communication problems—failures to listen and respond to others' points of view and concerns. How can problems be resolved when people and their views are often radically different?

2 What single model of conflict resolution do you feel holds the key to successful problem-solving in school settings? Are some models or systems, such as training via participation in "critical incident vignettes" (role-playing crisis situations), more effective than others?

3 What strategies and techniques to bring opposing groups together have not worked well, in terms of your own experience in school, business, and other settings? Explain, with examples if possible, though avoiding assessment of blame.

4 Which groups (for example, coaches or members of the counseling department) reveal the *fewest* numbers of inter- and intrapersonal

school conflicts? Why do these groups seem exempt from disputes, disagreements, and problems?

5 Must each year begin with an inservice devoted to conflict resolution, using disinterested consultants? How can professional staff members maintain progress in effective communication strategies and conflict resolution all year long?

Comments

The problems in virtually all professional settings reside not in knowledge bases but in interpersonal conflicts. Encouraging effective communication strategies and harmonious problem-solving are valuable skills for school administrators. Are research-based studies of school conflicts useful? Recall educational administration courses and recommendations about strategies and models for dealing with conflict resolution. What guiding principles for effective problem-solving can you offer from your own experience? Is it necessary to bring in outside consultants to train school professionals? Are retreats outside school settings the answer? Instead, must everyone commit to changing their behaviors, their views, and priorities?

PERFORMANCE OBJECTIVE
THE ADMINISTRATOR FACILITATES
PROCESSES AND ENGAGES IN
ACTIVITIES ENSURING THAT
—Effective communication skills are used.

Case Study 82

A number of communication issues have drawn your attention to and made you concerned about the quality of communications generated in the district. You wonder whether a communications policy might be necessary, one that clarifies the expectations of the administration and board. The tone and style of written documents in the district must reflect an optimistic, positive philosophy and the commitment to the personal involvement in the education of each student in the school. The following circumstances/issues have prompted your concern.

- An overwhelmingly negative tone characterizes special mid-quarter reports sent by teachers to parents and guardians. Note: Many of these begin with the flat statement such as "Todd is failing P.E."
- The student handbook also seems very negative, with its rules and penalties. The emphasis is more on warning students than welcoming them to school and introducing all the services and opportunities available to them.
- Local newspaper coverage of the board meetings seems geared to reporting the conflicts and emphasizing somewhat negative issues. Of course, sports events are the exceptions, but what about the rest of the academic program? What steps can the district take to inform the community of the district's mission and goals, to let everyone know the commitment to quality education that is evident schoolwide?
- Letters from the guidance and the dean's office are bound by legal constraints, and yet they seem equally informational and negative, if not cold. What about documents that notify parent/guardians about excessive tardies, internal and external suspensions, and minor disciplinary actions? How can these be anything but negative?

Discussion Questions

1 Does it really matter how a mid-quarter report sounds to the readers, the parents and guardians who receive them? Putting yourself in the place of the recipient, generate a short list of your expectations. Then, suggest guidelines for teachers who write and send the reports.

2 What is the purpose of the student handbook, and is it a guide as well as a "public relations" opportunity? Should a district be concerned about effective wording in view of students who may or may not care, many of whom simply discard the handbook?

3 What specific steps can be taken to "feed" the local media with background about the good things going on in the school?

4 Suggest sample sentences that should appear in letters about tardies, suspensions and counselor concerns.

Comments

A district's communications policy often states the district philosophy and mission and reflects the spirit of the school(s). A policy prioritizes the expectations for clear, concise, helpful and positively worded documents. It presents models of effectively worded documents. Also, teachers of business writing at the university level can speak to school personnel about techniques and strategies to use when writing. They might present an explanation of effective business writing skills applied to educational documents at faculty or inservice meetings. Techniques that engage the reader and create a neutral, businesslike tone or a feeling of goodwill involve readers in the message and pave the way toward compliance. However, is this additional responsibility asking too much from already overburdened faculty and staff members?

Note: Teachers and school staff members remain somewhat isolated from developments in business. One development is the attention to writing effective documents, including memos, reports, sales pieces, customer letters, and newsletters. These documents reach the school's audiences daily, parent/guardians, community members, and young adults.

PERFORMANCE OBJECTIVE

THE ADMINISTRATOR FACILITATES
PROCESSES AND ENGAGES IN
ACTIVITIES ENSURING THAT
—There is effective use of technology to
   manage school operations.

Case Study 83

When Arnold Matlock came to Brendel West High School, he found the staff mired in a nontechnological mode. "Sure we have got computers," said Sara Jenkins, his secretary. "The superintendent's office sent three of them over not more than a year ago. They are still in boxes in the storage room."

"Tell me," he said with a chuckle, "you ladies are not still using carbon paper, are you?"

"Oh no!" said Mrs. Jenkins, failing to see the principal's humor. "We use a copy machine," she replied with pride.

"I think, Mrs. Jenkins, that you and your staff need some inservice to get you up to speed on computer technology," said the principal as he tried to hide his surprise and his frustration. "I think, with a little training, you will find computers to be an indispensable part of your office equipment. I cannot believe that you were given computers and expected to use them without training. I will see that a series of training sessions is set up for you and the other people in our office. We need to bring Brendel West into the twenty-first century. I feel certain that once all of you become accustomed to computers, the staff will wonder how they ever got along without them. Some day, in the not-too-distant future, I envision us being able to do class scheduling, attendance taking and tracking, as well as discipline tracking, and, of course, report writing. We will be effective, Mrs. Jenkins, and I believe that we will be able to work smarter, too."

"I will tell you the truth, Mr. Matlock. We were all apprehensive about using these new computers. All of us come from an era when computers were not around."

"I understand your concern, Mrs. Jenkins, but I assure you that if you give technology a chance, you will wonder how you ever got along without it. I know we can improve the performance of this school 100 percent."

Discussion Questions

1 Do you agree with the manner in which the superintendent's office provided computers to the high school?

2 What would have been an appropriate way to introduce the staff to computers to ensure their proper usage?

3 Do you think Mr. Matlock's handling of Mrs. Jenkins and the office staff was appropriate?

4 Do you think that Mr. Matlock's goals for computer usage were too ambitious?

5 Do you think that inservice sessions for the staff instigated by the principal was an appropriate remedy to ensure compliance with the use of computers?

6 How would you go about allaying the office staff's fear of computer usage?

7 What would you have done to use computers to improve performance in the areas of attendance, discipline, and report writing?

8 In your school, how are computers used for managing school operations? What other types of technology do you use? Are there areas of operations for which you could use technology but currently do not?

9 Computers are costly. How can you defend spending money on computers, especially if they are soon out of date? Have computers allowed you to reduce staff and save money, or have you had to hire people who had computer skills, thereby increasing your spending?

10 How have you used technology for communications in the school district? Has this been worth the cost?

PERFORMANCE OBJECTIVE

THE ADMINISTRATOR FACILITATES
PROCESSES AND ENGAGES IN
ACTIVITIES ENSURING THAT
—Fiscal resources of the school are
  managed responsibly, efficiently, and
  effectively.

Case Study 84

"Mrs. Magee is at it again," said the secretary as Mrs. Beene walked into the outer office.

"What do you mean *again?*" asked Mrs. Beene as she began to go through the inter-office mail. The secretary handed her an invoice filled with items that she had purchased from an educational catalog that all of the faculty had received in the mail.

"I do not remember authorizing any of these purchases," said Mrs. Beene as she examined the invoice. "I do not see any purchase order number on this."

The secretary shook her head and smiled. "That is because you did not authorize it, and Mrs. Magee never bothers to get a purchase order.

She has ordered several sets of books for her classroom as well as posters and several other visual aids.''

Mrs. Beene shook her head. She could feel anger rising in her throat as she directed the secretary to contact the company and cancel the order. She told the secretary to refuse the shipment if the cancellation was too late.

Later that afternoon, Mrs. Beene confronted Mrs. Magee, an elementary teacher with 32 years of experience. ''I just received an invoice for $700.00 that was not authorized. Why did you order all those materials?''

Mrs. Magee peered over her bifocals as she looked up from the mounds of paper on her desk. ''I ordered the materials because my students needed them,'' she said simply.

Her answer was given in such a manner that Mrs. Beene felt as if she was being dismissed. Again, she felt her anger rising and her face becoming red.

''I appreciate your desire to do what is best for your students; however, you simply cannot order items without going through the proper procedures. We must all strive to function responsibly, efficiently, and effectively. I cannot authorize this order to be processed. In fact, this one order would break my school supply budget, Mrs. Magee.''

Mrs. Magee stood up and looked at Mrs. Beene incredulously. ''You mean you are canceling my order? I cannot believe it.''

''I am and I did,'' said Mrs. Beene resolutely. ''You need to understand that I am the principal and that I run this school according to rules and regulations. It is about time that you realized it because this is not the first time you have tried to circumvent school procedures. If you cannot abide by the rules, you have two choices: resign or transfer. I have an obligation to the students, but I have a bigger obligation to the other staff members and this school.''

Discussion Questions

1 What type of procedures should be in place with regard to ordering materials?

2 How would you handle a veteran teacher like Mrs. Magee?

3 Do you believe Mrs. Magee was using her seniority to circumvent procedures?

4 Do you believe that Mrs. Beene behaved in an appropriate manner in dealing with Mrs. Magee?

5 As a principal, how would you ensure that other members of your teaching staff did not commit this same impropriety?

6 As a principal, which would you prefer: to give each teacher a set amount of money to spend, or to have all teachers request what they need from one school "pool" of money? If you were a teacher, which would you prefer? Does it make any difference whether we are talking about an elementary school or a high school?

PERFORMANCE OBJECTIVE

THE ADMINISTRATOR FACILITATES
PROCESSES AND ENGAGES IN
ACTIVITIES ENSURING THAT
—A safe, clean, and aesthetically pleasing
school environment is created and
maintained.

Case Study 85

When Sam Ornstein arrived at Maple Middle School during the first part of the summer, he was shocked at the condition of the building. The floors were filthy, locker doors were off their hinges, classroom furniture was broken, and the building had the unpleasant odor of fermenting sweat socks.

He immediately called in the lead custodian and told him that as the new principal, his expectations were to have a clean, safe, controlled learning environment where students and teachers could learn and teach. Mr. Ornstein was adamant that things would change at Maple Middle School.

Mr. Stevens, the custodian, had seen principals come and go during his 22 years in the building. He had been told many times before that changes had to be made, but he had never followed through and the demands and high expectations were always forgotten. He had no intention of behaving any differently just because Mr. Ornstein had arrived as the new principal.

Several weeks later, in the middle of October, Mr. Ornstein called Mr. Stevens in and explained that his wishes had not been carried out. None of the improvements they had discussed during that first meeting had been implemented. ''You have until the end of Christmas vacation to get this building into shape. I am going to be monitoring you and the other custodial staff. This building will be safe and clean, or you and your crew will be looking for other jobs.''

Mr. Stevens agreed, but January 6th saw no improvements. When Mr. Ornstein called the staff in and fired them, they were all shocked and angered at this injustice.

Discussion Questions

1 Do you think that Mr. Ornstein had too many expectations for Mr. Stevens and his custodial staff?

2 How important is it to maintain a clean and safe learning environment?

3 Was the custodial staff given ample opportunity to make improvements within the time period at Maple Middle School?

4 Was terminating the entire custodial staff too harsh a solution?

PERFORMANCE OBJECTIVE

THE ADMINISTRATOR FACILITATES
PROCESSES AND ENGAGES IN
ACTIVITIES ENSURING THAT
—A safe, clean, and aesthetically pleasing
   school environment is created and
   maintained.

Case Study 86

Note the examples that follow:

- A suburban high school district, in view of unexpected increases in student enrollment, breaks up several larger rooms for more classrooms. Paperboard and ineffective "soundproof" screens divide rooms. These temporary solutions, though they look finished, remain in place six years after the enrollment additions, with no plans for change. It is difficult for instructors and students in these rooms to avoid hearing what goes on in the class on the opposite side of the screen. Showing films or videotapes, for example, is nearly impossible. Complaints fail to bring changes, and teachers resort to taking turns, year by year, instructing classes in less-than-satisfactory, makeshift rooms. These were viewed as temporary solutions; however, the district has financial problems.

- A building renovation necessitates changes in the west wing of one high school. Thus, several classrooms have plastic sheet partitions for their back walls for an indefinite time period. Students can see and hear construction workers through the plastic, though it is heavy plastic, during all class periods. Workers try to confine buzzsaw and other machinery noise to bare minimums. White dust is a daily nuisance—it covers every room surface.

- An older high school building lacks air conditioning. Thus, in 90+ degree temperatures, the principal brings in two large, noisy fans for each classroom on the third floor. It is virtually impossible to hear anything in the room except for the loud fan motors. Students are almost out of control with the disruptive noise; many throw paper wads in the fans. Teachers are almost forced to assign worksheets and seatwork, instead of group, panel, and interactive classroom activities, for most of late August and all of September. There are no plans to install air conditioning in the district buildings, especially since significant financial challenges already exist.

- Much-needed roof and other repairs are taking place in the high school, and a structural beam falling to the floor grazes the head and back of a teacher who enters the building one morning. She is dazed and frightened, but does not request or require medical help. She reports to the office what happened, but no one seems concerned; she does not feel it is her responsibility to follow through with a formal complaint of any kind (she values the job security she has). But she is not able to teach effectively that day, realizing that except for her own quick reaction time, she might have been seriously injured. The area involved was not roped off; no signs warned of potential falling beams.

Discussion Questions

1 Comment on the specific problem in each of the examples described above. Suggest appropriate solutions for each.

2 How can an administrator direct and monitor school improvements so that teaching and learning proceed uninterrupted? Is it necessary for administrators to watch progress and remain with workers as they complete their jobs?

3 How does one prepare a faculty, staff, students, and parents for building repairs and renovations, if so indicated in school buildings?

4 Offer an inexperienced principal some useful guidelines about building improvements/renovations, if these have not surfaced in discussions about the questions above.

5 Describe how administrators can set goals and priorities in terms of creating and maintaining *a safe, clean, aesthetically pleasing school environment.* Doesn't every person's opinion of that italicized phrase differ? Is a survey necessary to determine the opinion of a majority of the school community? Is it necessary to hire an architect, if only for consultative purposes?

PERFORMANCE OBJECTIVE

THE ADMINISTRATOR FACILITATES
PROCESSES AND ENGAGES IN
ACTIVITIES ENSURING THAT
—A safe, clean, and aesthetically pleasing
  school environment is created and
  maintained.

Case Study 87

The principal has an appointment with someone she does not recall meeting. "I'm Glenda Morris," the visitor begins. "My son will be a freshman next year, and I've heard good and bad about this high school. Mr. Morris and I are prepared to make sacrifices to send our Norman to a private school, if necessary.'' The principal is about to speak, but it is obvious that Mrs. Morris has just begun.

Mrs. Morris continues: "I am first of all concerned about Norman's education; we want him to go to college. But is this a safe school? I read about your confiscating hunting guns from some students last year. I won't tolerate guns in my son's school. What kind of security do you have? Also, discipline. Is there good discipline in this school, or are classes up for grabs? I've heard rumors about some schools around here where it's just wild.'' There is a pause.

"Gangs. I don't want Norman exposed to anything having to do with gangs. Growing up is hard enough. And what about drugs? I've seen those kids in groups hanging around the outside of this building some mornings when I am on my way to work. They're up to no good, as I see it.''

Discussion Questions

1 Mrs. Morris targets the concerns of many community members, as well as parent/guardians: a good education, safety/security and weapons, discipline, gangs, and drug activity. How much might a principal reveal about school problems, including correcting misperceptions and/or describing strategies in place to deal with these issues? What would be a guide on discussing such issues?

2 If asked by a similarly concerned parent, describe your response to these issues, in light of circumstances in your own school.

3 How can a busy school leader be knowledgeable and keep updated about a variety of safety and security problems in the building, as well as discipline problems, gangs, and drug activity?

4 What steps should a principal new to the job take to assess the exact nature of the problems described above in a particular school? Note: many interview situations cause people to be on their best behaviors and to downplay or understate the severity of some problems. Also, are assessment techniques the same for experienced school administrators?

5 How would a new principal know that gangs may be a potential problem, especially if there is no evidence of slogans, certain forms

of address, hand salutes and gestures, and wearing/displaying specific colors? Might the principal feel safe in thinking that gangs are not a problem in the district?

6 How do administrators know when problems related to safety/security, discipline, drugs, and gang activity are no longer a concern? What steps can be taken to monitor activity in relation to all of these? For example, some students kept weapons locked in the trunks of their cars, parked in the school parking lot, and no one suspected they were there.

PERFORMANCE OBJECTIVE

THE ADMINISTRATOR FACILITATES
PROCESSES AND ENGAGES IN
ACTIVITIES ENSURING THAT
—Human resource functions support the
  attainment of school goals.

Case Study 88

"All you ever seem to want is more money and more staff," said Dr. North, the superintendent of Hillside Independent School District.

"You are absolutely right, Bud," countered George Beck, the junior/senior high school principal. "But you know as well as I do that an effective school program costs money and you have to have the proper staff. My requests for a school nurse and a social worker are not unreasonable."

"I know, George, but I answer to the board and to the community. You know full well they keep an eye on every dollar we spend."

"We are dealing with truly needy kids and our mission is to help them be successful. To me, Bud, that means being both physically and mentally healthy. You know I would not ask for these positions unless I truly felt they were extremely necessary."

"George, you know I agree with you, but what will I tell the board? We must keep the budget in line. Write up a proposal and I will see what I can do."

Discussion Questions

1 Should budget concerns impact on human resources needs?

2 Do you believe the principal truly needed the positions of full-time nurse and social worker?

3 Do you think the principal adequately stated the importance of his personnel needs?

4 Do you think the superintendent reacted too much to board pressures?

5 What would you have submitted to the superintendent if you were assigned to write the personnel proposal?

PERFORMANCE OBJECTIVE

THE ADMINISTRATOR FACILITATES
PROCESSES AND ENGAGES IN
ACTIVITIES ENSURING THAT
—Confidentiality and privacy of school
 records are maintained.

Case Study 89

Betty Ann and John Kramer had divorced after 10 years of marriage. They had two sons in Northfield Elementary School. About a year after the divorce, John came by the school office to talk to the principal, Mrs. Napier. "Mrs. Napier, I am John Kramer, and I came to school to check on my two kids. Since the divorce, I have not seen any of the report cards and do not know how they are doing in school. I see the kids now and again, but they don't say much about school. Betty Ann won't hardly talk to me about anything. I am still their father, and Betty Ann has not married again, so I feel I am entitled to know how they are doing here. I want to see their report cards for the past year and their attendance records. I used to have real good attendance records myself and got a certificate once."

Discussion Questions

1 What should Mrs. Napier do?
2 As the father, is John entitled to the records?
3 Does Mrs. Napier have to get permission from Betty Ann?
4 Do the courts enter into this issue at all?
5 Should the records have been sent to John instead of Betty Ann, or maybe to both of them?
6 Should the school district have a policy to deal with this issue? If so, what might it say?
7 Do we have to consult with attorneys just to show someone a report card for his/her own children?
8 Does privacy and confidentiality come into this case since it is a parent asking to see the records? Do parents (not divorced) have the right to see all school records of their own children? What constitutes "school records"?

Comments

Mrs. Napier probably needs to delay any decision unless the district has a policy and she already knows how it applies to this case. Otherwise, she may need to find out what the court decision was in the divorce: Who has legal custody? What does that custody concern? Is one party restricted from obtaining any information about the children?

CHAPTER 6

Standard 4 Case Studies

A school administrator is an educational leader who promotes the success of all students by collaborating with families and community members, responding to diverse community interests and needs, and mobilizing community resources.

PERFORMANCE OBJECTIVE

THE ADMINISTRATOR FACILITATES
PROCESSES AND ENGAGES IN
ACTIVITIES ENSURING THAT
—High visibility, active involvement, and
  communication with the larger community
  is a priority.

Case Study 90

In order to both support the educational program and increase her involvement in the community, the principal of District 200 contemplates her role and some changes that may be necessary. For example, weekly visiting as many classes as possible this year will allow the principal to know the academic program from the inside. In addition, talking informally with each teacher in the building will yield the perspective of each, especially with regard to concerns about particular students. However, community involvement is also indicated. The principal considers:

- writing a column for the local newspaper every other week, with updates on school activities, educational programs per department, changes in policy, etc.

165

- participating in the Chamber of Commerce's board and activities; also, evolving a new brochure to give real estate agents as part of their "Welcome to Clearview" literature
- joining the local service groups that meet weekly
- running an informational/public relations ad in the local business directory, highlighting the five outstanding features of the school (number of courses offered, computer-assisted programs, number of teachers with master's and doctorate degrees, list of special student services available, accreditation status)
- joining the local MADD chapter, eliciting their help in presenting alcohol awareness programs
- contacting local TV stations with inquiries about future programming, especially "In School Today" and "In School: Issues"
- offering to participate in Community Services Board meetings and activities

Discussion Questions

1 Do these activities accommodate the principal's goals for high visibility, involvement in, and communication with the community at large?

2 What specific activities do administrators in your district participate in to achieve this principal's goals?

3 What avenues for visibility, involvement, and communication has the principal overlooked?

4 What community leaders might the principal contact for further suggestions?

Comments

A school leader must weigh the benefits of increased involvement in community groups and activities to create high visibility and "continue the dialogue" as needed. Busy administrators need some guiding principles for involvement. How much time expended in these activities is "enough"? What indicates overinvolvement? How does one gauge the merits of the various alternatives available? Are there any that guarantee the results school leaders seek? Which involvements are more "social" and thus potential time wasters? Discussing a sharing of responsibilities among all school administrators in the district might be worthwhile, as well as bringing up the topic at the area administrators' monthly meetings.

PERFORMANCE OBJECTIVE

THE ADMINISTRATOR FACILITATES
PROCESSES AND ENGAGES IN
ACTIVITIES ENSURING THAT
—Relationships with community leaders are
  identified and nurtured.

Case Study 91

Bob, the current superintendent of a small-town school district, was visiting with the former superintendent, Ron Harley. After relaxing and discussing the previous night's basketball game, Bob said, "Ron, as you know, I have been having some problems lately—or maybe I should say I have had them ever since I came here a year or so ago. I don't seem to have the confidence of the people around here. They seem pleasant enough, but I don't think they realize what I am trying to do or how I am going about it. I make regular reports at the school board meetings, and the press manages to pick up some of my comments, though inaccurately at times. Do you have any suggestions? You were so well liked and admired here."

"Well, I don't know about that. I had my share of problems, too. It's just that when I retired, everyone seemed to remember the good things—which I appreciate. You have to remember, Bob, that you have only been here for about one year. It takes some time for a new superintendent to gain the people's confidence. Bob, have you taken the time to get to know the community leaders? You know: the president of the Chamber of Commerce and the heads of the civic organizations like the Lions Club, the Kiwanis, and Rotary International. And, have you joined any of these groups?"

"Well, I have not had much time to do this," Bob replied. "Do you think this is a good idea?"

"It is essential, Bob! If you expect to be successful in this town, you have to identify the leaders and build a relationship with each of them. I can help you by telling you who they are and what positions they are likely to take. Then, the rest is up to you.''

Discussion Questions

1 Do you agree with Ron? Why or why not?
2 If you were Ron, what leaders would you discuss with Bob?
3 What do you think Ron meant by saying he would tell Bob the leaders and ''positions they are likely to take''?
4 What other suggestions would you make to Bob to help him develop relationships with community leaders?
5 Should a superintendent join civic clubs? If there are three or four in town, which should Bob join? Should principals join such clubs?
6 The assumption seems to be that community leaders are those who have been elected to head up a club or organization. Is that always the situation? Can you think of leaders who do not hold such positions?

Comments

Besides using Ron's advice (which is good), Bob can do other things. Depending on the size of the town, Bob can go around to area businesses and introduce himself to the manager or owner of each. As far as which club to join, it may depend on whether he has been a member in a previous town. Also, a board member or other administrator may suggest a club that is appropriate. Sometimes each principal is associated with a different club. One of the authors was once a superintendent in a district that included seven communities, each with its own set of organizations. The board recommended that the superintendent not join any club in order to avoid the appearance of neglecting all the rest of them. Instead, some of the principals joined clubs in the area where their schools were located. Bob will have the opportunity to speak to all of the clubs in his area, whether a member or not, and can use those times to develop relationships with members. In a small town, it is also wise to get to know the ministers, bank officers, and the fire and police chiefs.

PERFORMANCE OBJECTIVE
_____

THE ADMINISTRATOR FACILITATES
PROCESSES AND ENGAGES IN
ACTIVITIES ENSURING THAT
—Information about family and community
concerns, expectations, and needs is used
regularly.
_____

Case Study 92

The principal realizes that a commitment to keep in touch with the community is very important. She creates a survey to distribute to all district parent/guardians, with both check-off and open-ended questions. She also reviews the local demographic studies and is an interested participant in the meetings of the community adolescent center (a physical and mental health care facility with tutorials, a jobs network system, and a referral group). A dialogue is necessary to understand community expectations, and the principal has started an open phone line several hours each week (so far, no one has called). She reads the local newspaper each day and brings up issues at the administrative council meetings, as needed. In addition, she plans to set up luncheon meetings with five local businesses, the area's largest employers, in order to gain their perspectives.

Discussion Questions

1 How else can a school leader gain information about family concerns that impact their children and the school? Note: Some people are overwhelmingly reluctant to share problems, feeling these should be kept confidential.

2 What are good sources to pursue in becoming aware of community concerns, especially in view of the diversity of views present?

3 Are board meetings the only avenues parent/guardians and community members use to pinpoint their expectations and concerns?

4 Using your own experience, relate other sources of information that reflect the concerns of all the stakeholders in a community.

Comments

Information from a variety of sources is necessary in order to survey a wide sampling of individuals and groups. In this way, community concerns and problems may surface. What sources do administrators in your district use to obtain this kind of information? What sources might a school leader avoid? Are school board members helpful and knowledgeable in this information gathering? How could board members contribute to information gathering? What about parent organizations?

PERFORMANCE OBJECTIVE

THE ADMINISTRATOR FACILITATES
PROCESSES AND ENGAGES IN
ACTIVITIES ENSURING THAT
—There is outreach to different business,
religious, political, and service agencies
and organizations.

Case Study 93

An administrative team meeting reveals that school leaders feel they need to access community resources more effectively this year. Individual administrators express various priorities:

- Member churches in the township religious council will stage holiday food, clothing, and toy collections this year (students might help publicize the events, as well as collect and distribute donations).
- Local nursing homes and hospitals need volunteers to take residents and patients on walks—or just socialize with them for awhile (students as well as residents and patients benefit from time spent this way).
- The Chamber of Commerce and Rotary members might discuss the global marketplace and forecast job and career trends, as well as explain their own career paths since high school to interested students (these are potential mentors and network

sources for students, especially seniors undecided about their future careers).

- The League of Women Voters needs to address students and encourage their understanding of participation in local and national elections, even though this is a one-party region, as it has been historically.
- An adolescent health care center is now open downtown, but no one really knows much about their services and staff (giving students another option if they need help is usually a good idea).
- The tutorial phone line is underway; tutor/student meetings take place in the high school library most evenings. However, personnel involved might review a few of their "success stories" and get testimonials from students who have used their services.
- Teen Scene, an informal coffeehouse located downtown, was once a gathering place, supervised by volunteer adults. It provided old but comfortable chairs and a place for teens to talk. Is there a need for and interest in Teen Scene again?

Discussion Questions

1 What other services/functions might the groups listed above offer area high school students? Can one quantify the results of cooperation between these groups and the high school? How can one assess the effectiveness of exchanges between the groups listed and the high school?

2 Suggest how school districts that you are familiar with have utilized the talents and offerings of yet other community groups and resources, commenting especially on untapped sources, if not mentioned for reactions to Question #1 above.

3 What objections do you anticipate that some parent/guardians and community members might have to such exchanges and outreach? Have community members voiced objections that you know of related to outreach programs? Should a district drop the outreach/ resources exchange idea if, say, five or more objections surface once programs begin?

4 Comment on whether a school needs an oversight committee or a designated school administrator-facilitator to monitor the use of

community groups and outreach programs. Advise an interested potential facilitator about the need for and value of outreach connections, while warning about possible detrimental factors. For example, can the whole program effort get out of hand and become uncontrollable? What steps can be taken to ensure good experiences for everyone involved?

5 Is it necessary to involve teachers in community outreach efforts? Is it necessary to connect all activities to classwork and district goals and objectives?

Comments

Connecting schools with communities is an objective of many school districts' reform efforts. The desire to increase students' educational opportunities is well intentioned. And yet, some cautionary advice seems necessary. Some parents, for example, may view these attempts as diverting students from academic responsibilities; others feel their children's services, if rendered, demand recompense. A judicious administrator prepares carefully for community outreach programs, researches the topic, and, possibly, conducts opinion surveys. As a result, school leaders can establish parameters for involvement. These should not be hasty decisions.

PERFORMANCE OBJECTIVE

THE ADMINISTRATOR FACILITATES
PROCESSES AND ENGAGES IN
ACTIVITIES ENSURING THAT
—Credence is given to individuals and
  groups whose values and opinions may
  conflict.

Case Study 94

Up to this point, one suburban district has been relatively unaffected by diversity in its school population. However, things have changed. A strong and vocal group of religious evangelicals is represented in the community, people deeply committed to their faith and exceptionally clear-sighted about their own point of view. Representatives of the group are unyielding in their agenda to "protect students" and censor all learning materials used in the schools. In addition, a wave of Asian-American and East Indian families has come to live in this prosperous area, looking for a good life and good schools. Many of these parent/guardians are dual-income professionals working at an international conglomerate's regional office, located in the next town. In addition, children associated with "the hill people" currently represent almost 10% of the school populace; a large group of migrant workers enjoy employment almost year-round due to the mostly balmy climate and an abundance of nearby factories and businesses. Although the latter group of parent/guardians also wants their children to have a good education, they are, for the most part, uninvolved in school district matters and suspicious of bureaucracies. They do not necessarily understand the processes and terminology of contemporary education, though they realize their children have always had difficulties adjusting to "the rich kids" in "the rich school."

Discussion Questions

1 How do school leaders open the dialogue with all their constituents, especially those maintaining diverse traditions, customs, beliefs, and lifestyles? A wide range of cultures are represented in this school district. How can schools seek out and welcome input from all who have children in school?

2 Are special community spokespersons, advocates, or representatives of these groups necessary to ensure equal and fair treatment? Would a cultural board to articulate special interests be advisable?

3 Is it a school's business to encourage respect for all people and their cultures? Although lip service is given to *respect* and *tolerance,* how does that translate into behaviors when it comes to academic learning? How is it possible to protect the rights of all groups regarding educational opportunities, as well as emphasize individual responsibilities?

4 What steps can a school district take to protect its own traditions while accommodating a changing school populace? How might the school continue to offer the same strong academic program that has established its reputation?

5 School officials did not necessarily anticipate the changes that would occur in the population and the communities surrounding the district. How might school leaders recognize and prepare for problems that may already exist?

6 What changes in programs, policies, rules and regulations do you foresee for this district? What changes are you aware of in school districts you are familiar with? How have school leaders adapted to changes in the population of the community, as well as other economic realities that impact families and schools?

7 What guidelines can you offer school leaders about the complexities of educating diverse school populations and communicating with all those in a community who are interested in schools and educational opportunities?

PERFORMANCE OBJECTIVE

THE ADMINISTRATOR FACILITATES
PROCESSES AND ENGAGES IN
ACTIVITIES ENSURING THAT
—The school and community serve one
  another as resources.

Case Study 95

The first meeting of the administrative council team reviews opportunities for expanding students' academic and extracurricular success. Their goal is to reach out to more sources related to the ability of both school and community to serve one another as resources.

The community serves the school district as a resource in the following ways:

- Businesses give donations—prizes for Homecoming, raffles and lock-in prom night; also materials for decorating downtown store windows for Homecoming and various sports throughout the school year.
- Businesses offer materials plus signs and banners advertising sport season schedules and tournaments.
- The city allows use of community pool for frosh-soph team practices and swim club activities.

- Membership invites participation in the annual art guild tent fair, offering a section for student entries in art, photography, sculpture, and mixed media.
- Businesses provide locations for class car wash fund-raisers.
- The Chamber of Commerce encourages participation in local fall apple festival.

The school district serves the community as a resource in the following ways:

- Band, orchestra, and chorus join the local parades and celebrations.
- The Fun Run/Walk/Stroll is hosted by teachers to contribute to the Community Chest, the annual fund drive, as well as to school causes.
- Interested students serve as hospital volunteers and docents for the local museum.
- Students volunteer help for the spring basket project, which serves nursing home residents and children in day care settings.
- A holiday food drive is sponsored by the Interfaith Council; sports teams collect donations and distribute them.
- Adult education courses at school target many skills and interests; also, discount sports-events tickets are given to interested senior citizen community members.

Discussion Questions

1 What other community interests and needs might the administrators target in order to expand student opportunities? Give specific examples of how communities serve as resources for schools in terms of your experience.

2 Suggest a suitable example that might cause school leaders to mobilize community resources; for example, programs to prevent teen pregnancies or deter drug and alcohol abuse and sponsoring various speakers and special videos.

3 Convince dubious community members who are attending a school board meeting that the school and community exchange, each acting as a resource, is a legitimate goal for both.

4 How has your school district served the community as a resource? How does the community serve your school(s)? In what ways would you like to see an expansion for either or both?

5 How does an administrator assess the worth of mutual exchanges? Give specific examples, as needed.

Comments

Mutual benefit results when schools and communities join forces and expand opportunities for students. Students may benefit from participating in various phases of community life. At times, community members are too far removed from students and school business. One important goal is encouraging dissemination of information about what is going on in the school district. Understanding the wide range of possibilities in the connection between schools and communities begins with specifying examples of actual resource exchanges that you know have been successful.

PERFORMANCE OBJECTIVE

THE ADMINISTRATOR FACILITATES
PROCESSES AND ENGAGES IN
ACTIVITIES ENSURING THAT
—Available community resources are secured
  to help the school solve problems and
  achieve goals.

Case Study 96

A group of school administrators recognize the value of community resources, and this year they agree they must actively recruit or pursue these resources. Some of their concerns include

- availability of part-time jobs for eligible/needy students
- career seminars that review a wide range of careers and occupations as well as specifics about the changing marketplace
- additional counseling services, including topics such as eating disorders counseling, self-esteem, self-confidence building, and study skills and motivational counseling

- community members to serve as year-long tutors for interested students who need supplemental help
- nonuniversity education, including technical training and two-year program alternatives (with or without certificates); internships in trade occupations
- computer learning, computer applications for business and industry

The administrators discuss what is available in their mid-size rural community and what to do about the lack of large corporations, businesses, and industries. The community does have a Chamber of Commerce whose membership includes almost 250 businesses, mostly small but some mid-size. In addition, there is an area community college and new youth services center downtown.

This area has abundant lakes and attracts many boaters and people who enjoy fishing. How might area hotels and motels, besides recreational facilities, become a school and student resource? Consider the following that are significant in this community: a large construction company, a (construction) truss builder, a rehabilitative service, and a group of lawn service, landscapers, and nursery owners. How might each of those be utilized?

Discussion Questions

1 What specific presentations and programs can the administrators make to the representatives of these resources that target their concerns and would be useful to high school students?

2 Given what they consider are the "limited" resources of the community, suggest other avenues they might pursue that target their concerns.

3 How can the largest factory in the area (Eat-em Cookies and Crackers) serve as a resource for the school and its students, besides conducting plant tours?

4 What parameters or guides might the administrators give potential resources? What kind of contacts would yield results—letters of inquiry? visits to facilities? phone calls? Suggest an approach for reluctant administrators.

Comments

A school district's academic program can be strengthened by anticipating and addressing concerns common to young adults. Providing for their successful futures reaches beyond a sound academic program. Today's world is complex, and students must be prepared to choose satisfying careers with job availability. In addition, they must know what companies need in terms of skilled employees. Today's schools must consider a new imperative: reaching beyond the classroom and into the marketplace.

PERFORMANCE OBJECTIVE

THE ADMINISTRATOR FACILITATES
PROCESSES AND ENGAGES IN
ACTIVITIES ENSURING THAT
—Available community resources are secured
  to help the school solve problems and
  achieve goals.

Case Study 97

"Have you seen the latest figures?" Mrs. Gomez asked the principal as she laid the report on his desk. Raul Ramirez looked up, "What figures? What report?"

"I am speaking of the dropout rates of our students. I think many of them are teen pregnancies. It is not a pleasant picture."

"Okay, Mrs. Gomez. You are our head counselor, what can we do to lessen the dropout rate at our school? I know the health teachers have tried to discuss it in their classes, but these figures suggest they are not being effective. I also know that you and your staff have tried individual counseling to no avail."

"Mr. Ramirez, perhaps the students do not pay any attention to us. Perhaps we need to get members of the community involved. Maybe listening to someone from the outside might be a help. It certainly could not hurt."

"What do you propose we do, Mrs. Gomez?"

"I propose that we contact people our students look up to, including athletes, television personalities, and former students who have been successful. Maybe we should include those students who have dropped out and who wish they could have had a second chance."

"Since I am the principal, I am putting you in charge."

Discussion Questions

1 Do you believe that teachers can be an effective deterrent to teenage problems?

2 How effective is a high school counseling staff?

3 Should Mr. Ramirez have been more aware of the problems involving his students?

4 Do you feel that involving unsuccessful students in this program would deter potential student problems?

5 Are there any other low-cost or no-cost solutions that the school could initiate?

PERFORMANCE OBJECTIVE

THE ADMINISTRATOR FACILITATES
PROCESSES AND ENGAGES IN
ACTIVITIES ENSURING THAT
—Partnerships are established with area
business, institutions of higher education,
and community groups to strengthen
programs and support school goals.

Case Study 98

Margo Johnson, the high school counselor, hung up the phone and sadly shook her head. She had just been speaking with Mr. Carruthers, a local business owner, who called to complain about the quality of the work study students Central High School's business department had been sending him. She tried to be an advocate for the department and its teachers, but she knew that Mr. Carruthers was correct when he said the students were not able to function in an actual business setting. She knew the Central teachers were unfamiliar with current trends and that much of the coursework was antiquated by modern business standards.

After some deliberation, she went to Mrs. Wagner, the principal of Central, to discuss both the call and her own concerns about the curriculum. Mrs. Wagner tended to agree with the counselor's conclusions. It was at this point that Mrs. Wagner contacted the superintendent to inform her of the problem and to seek her guidance.

The problem was twofold, an aging staff and lack of funds. Mrs. Wagner and the superintendent decided that outside help was in order. If businesses were concerned, perhaps they needed more input into curricular decisions. Several business leaders were contacted and asked to come to Central to discuss concerns and to suggest possible improvements. These business leaders were given both the current curriculum and an overview of the financial situation that was plaguing Central High and the entire district. These business leaders were asked to form a partnership and to provide help in the form of advisory committees, as well as aid in the form of donated computers and other items. Additionally, the community college was contacted, and an effort was made to articulate a curriculum between the high school and postgraduate classes in business. Several of the instructors volunteered to serve on the Central High advisory committee.

Discussion Questions

1 Do you think that Mr. Carruthers was fair in his assessment that the business students were unprepared?

2 Should Mrs. Wagner have contacted the superintendent, or should she simply have created the business advisory committee on her own?

3 How does it look to businesses to be asked for help in providing funds and materials?

4 Why should the community college be involved in a high school advisory committee?

5 Were the teachers in the business department at fault for what had prompted Mr. Carruthers' telephone call to the counselor?

PERFORMANCE OBJECTIVE
THE ADMINISTRATOR FACILITATES
PROCESSES AND ENGAGES IN
ACTIVITIES ENSURING THAT
—Community youth family services are
integrated with school programs.

Case Study 99

Rita Cosgrove, director of Family Services, was meeting with the district principals. "I appreciate all of you taking the time to meet with me about mutual concerns. Let me get right to the point. As you may know from the local paper, my budget has been cut by the town board. As a result, I feel we will have a hard time maintaining all the programs that we have now—in fact, we really can't keep them all, let alone expand to some of the other programs that our children and families need. I need help from the schools. I know you can't give me money, but maybe you can help with facilities, personnel needs, supplies and equipment. I'm not sure what else. We need to offer these services or the community, including the schools, will suffer."

Jan Berry, an elementary principal, replied, "We all know that your staff has done a great job in the community, but I am not sure exactly what we could do to help. And I wonder if there are any legal problems in providing some of these things to you. What do the rest of you think?"

Discussion Questions

1 Consider the legal question Jan raised. For each of these requests, do you see any legal problems?

- shared use of facilities
- shared use of personnel
- giving supplies to family services to use
- giving equipment to family services to borrow
- using school information services to advertise family services

- using time during school for appointments for family services
- other requests

2 What are the advantages and disadvantages of integrating youth family services and the school program?

3 How could family services counselors work with school counselors in this cooperative arrangement?

4 Is there any reason to have the school attorney involved? What might be put into writing about the arrangement?

5 Following up on this concept of integration of community programs and school programs, are there other community programs that could be integrated to benefit both programs? Recreational, scouts, etc.

PERFORMANCE OBJECTIVE

THE ADMINISTRATOR FACILITATES
PROCESSES AND ENGAGES IN
ACTIVITIES ENSURING THAT
—Community stakeholders are treated
  equitably.

Case Study 100

Under the "Comments from the Public" item on the agenda of the board of education, a young high school student was pleading with the board not to eliminate the job of one of his teachers. This action had been recommended by the superintendent due to a decline in enrollment, especially in the area taught by this teacher.

"She really is a good teacher, and she should not have to lose her job just because the school has fewer students. It just isn't fair."

"That's life," the board president said. "Life isn't always fair. You had better get used to it now, young man."

Lucy Potter, another board member who was somewhat embarrassed by this exchange, looked down at her agenda to see what other items were coming before the board. She then turned to the superintendent's confidential memorandum to the board members, giving his recommendations to the board. In part, it read:

1 "Comments from the Public"—While we should allow people to express their views, we cannot let them take over our meeting. Also, it really bothers me when people speak who are not residents or parents of our students. The union president, who does not even live in the school district, always wants to say his piece. Also, as you know, we have been working on and discussing how we can change the grade levels that are in each building. Since we have not come to a final conclusion, I do not think it is helpful to have people speak to us with suggestions that we have already rejected. It is just of waste of our time.

2 "Use of School Facilities"—You will note that we have been asked to allow the Lutheran Church to use one of our rooms at the high school for a book sale. I recommend that this not be approved. Although we do let the Methodist Church hold bean suppers here each month, that is different. This has been allowed for years, and several of you even serve the meals for the church. The Lutheran Church book sale might have books that are religious in nature, and we don't want to be accused of emphasizing one church's views over another. Beans are just beans!

3 "Assignment of District Funds to Banks"—Every year at this time we must choose a bank for our deposits. I contacted the two banks in town and both have applied through the regular legal procedures to be depositories for our funds. In order to give each bank some business, I recommend that we do as we have always done: deposit all district funds in the First National Bank and have the high school deposit its extracurricular accounts in the Citizen's Trust Bank for the year.

4 "Special Presentation"—I have invited the Democratic representative for our district to talk to us on a topic of his choice. (If we ever get a Republican elected here, I will consider inviting him, but I may retire before that happens!)

Discussion Questions

1 What does the Performance Standard mean by "stakeholders"? Who is included in that term?

2 What does it mean to treat them all "equitably"?

3 Make a list of all of the examples in the case study where stakeholders may not have been treated equitably.

4 For each example, how could the board or superintendent have handled the situation differently?

Comments

Obviously, the board president could have been more sensitive to the student who felt badly about his teacher's dismissal. Here are some comments on the superintendent's recommendations:

1 Members of the public cannot be allowed to take over a meeting. The "public" nature of the board meeting means that the public is entitled to hear the deliberations and decisions of the board. It does not mean that the public is entitled to comment on each item at length or participate in the deliberations. However, most boards today *do* want to allow the public to express their opinions to the board, and the board should allow people who are not residents to speak if they have something relevant to say and do not take up too much time. Finally, the board cannot expect everyone to say things that agree with the board's position.

2 If the school district allows one community group to use the schools, it should allow other community groups to use the school. In fact, in legal cases where a board would not allow a group (i.e., PTA) to use the school because it did not like its views, and the courts said they had to treat all groups the same. Not wanting to promote a particular religion is a good idea, but prohibiting a book sale while allowing a bean supper is not being consistent. A district should have a policy for use of the building, including any charges, and be consistent in its application.

3 The bank recommendation may appear fair on the surface, but the district funds are huge in comparison to the high school activity funds. To put them in the same bank yearly is not fair to the other bank unless the board can declare a very good reason for doing so.

4 The board should not invite just one political party to speak to them, even if the other has not elected a representative in years. Besides, note that the speaker is choosing his own topic.

PERFORMANCE OBJECTIVE
THE ADMINISTRATOR FACILITATES
PROCESSES AND ENGAGES IN
ACTIVITIES ENSURING THAT
—Diversity is recognized and valued.

Case Study 101

The school principal, Mr. Mony, finished his speech to the Rotary Club: "In conclusion, in this community and in my school, we feel that diversity is important. Both the community and school have people of various color and ethnic backgrounds, and it is important for us to remember that. We need to value this diversity and let it shine throughout the school and the town. We have certain days at school to honor people of different backgrounds, and we encourage them to discuss the past achievements, culture, clothes, songs, and dances of their race or ethnic background. This is the American way! Only in America! Thank you very much for having me here today."

The Rotarian in charge of the meeting asked for questions, and one man jumped up immediately stating, "I have to disagree with you. Here is a coin I just pulled out of my pocket. It says *E Pluribus Unum* on this and on all U.S. coins. It doesn't say *E Pluribus Pluribus!* This great country was founded on the idea that many different people come here and then they all become Americans. We are spending too much time dwelling on the past of all these groups when we should be concentrating on becoming one people—Americans. And schools should spend time on teaching these kids to read, not on how to dance and sing songs from a hundred years ago in a foreign country. I'm sorry I got so excited, but that is how I feel."

Discussion Questions

1 If you were Mr. Mony, how would you respond to this "question"?
2 Does the questioner have a point or is his statement just a racist opinion?
3 Should schools spend academic time reviewing the cultures of different groups?

4 Should schools encourage "becoming one people" or "maintaining differences"? Is there any middle ground?

5 What is the "American way"?

6 Is the melting pot theory out of date?

PERFORMANCE OBJECTIVE

THE ADMINISTRATOR FACILITATES
PROCESSES AND ENGAGES IN
ACTIVITIES ENSURING THAT
—Effective media relations are developed
and maintained.

Case Study 102

With the district budgetary limits as they are, the high school principal realizes that creating "effective media relations" will be *his* job. The principal tries to think like a public relations representative in order to create, develop, and maintain good ties with the media. Let's face it, schools need good publicity these days, especially in this community which seems to have a disproportionate share of very vocal critics.

If I were a "PR man," how would I approach the media, the principal asks himself. First, I would invite media representatives to the school, then take them on a tour of the building. We then might meet in the conference room for coffee; I need to explain the importance of getting the word out about "exciting new things" going on in educating district students. I can get them involved with these strategies:

1 Fact sheets—I will offer the local newspaper single sheets of specifics on various aspects of school life, including new curriculum choices, changes in the open campus policy, refinishing the gym floors, the school's partnerships with local businesses, etc. This will be a weekly priority, and my office will originate these publications.

2 Press releases—The journalism classes and the journalism teacher may be interested in writing monthly press releases on stories of general interest, unrelated to sports events. For example, many community members may be unaware of students' efforts with service projects. The foreign language department sponsors the yearly food drive for the needy. There are many other newsworthy

items: health education now includes a powerful new antismoking unit, various social science classes are involved in sensitizing students to the dynamics of cultural diversity, and home economics classes have changed drastically in the last five years or so. These are only a few feature story possibilities—there are dozens like them.

3 Student aides—The local radio station needs a cadre of interested students who are willing to organize, classify, and shelve tapes, to file printed materials, to type reports and programs, and to complete a host of other tasks, especially on the weekends. Broadcasters are eager to have student input on a variety of issues that are of interest to high school students, since management is considering a "Teen Scene" show from 3–5 P.M. every week. Free publicity for news items related to school events and activities might be offered; students might gain an invaluable perspective from their behind-the-scenes experience.

4 Student observers—Audiovisual club members have expressed interest in interviewing personnel at the local TV station. Though there is no formal program, we might begin an internship-style arrangement that would allow students to participate in various aspects of broadcast journalism. Other A-V club members are interested in the technical aspects of productions.

Creating ties to the local media benefits the school and the media, he reasons. Our school deserves some good press and a chance to brag a little as we inform community members about the kind of educational opportunities we offer students. The media gets a lot of information about our school, a local source of pride and a resource everyone can be proud of.

As far as maintaining those good relationships with the media, I know I will continue the Fact Sheets as long as they are accepted by the newspaper. We will try the press releases from journalism classes as a pilot program, as we will with the radio station student aides and the student observers at the TV station. We have never done any of these things before, and it is time to try some new approaches. We may even soften up the community critics as well as the local education reporters. Just wait until they see what we're doing for students in this district! We'll flood them with "good news."

Discussion Questions

1 Is the principal realistic in his hope that covering all the media bases will do more good than harm? Note that he will reach out to the local newspaper as well as radio and TV stations.

2 Comment on these impressions: The media is interested in only scandals and sensationalism and local education reporters are more committed to building their own reputations and careers rather than advertising good things about the local schools.

3 What suggestions would you offer to the principal in order to ensure the wisest use of time and effort on the part of the administrator, the journalism teacher, journalism classes, and other students interested in these involvements with the media?

4 Offer other strategies to create and maintain good relationships with local newspapers, radio, and TV stations. Use specifics from your own experiences or those experiences that you have heard or read about, especially in your own district. Has the principal overlooked any other media sources?

5 What specifics should guide pilot programs that connect interested students with the local media? Are there any precautions that might be observed? Any legal issues?

6 Anticipate parent/guardian reactions to their children's involvements in media operations. How may community members react to these involvements?

7 Do the benefits for the media outweigh the time and effort media specialists may spend working with students?

PERFORMANCE OBJECTIVE

THE ADMINISTRATOR FACILITATES
PROCESSES AND ENGAGES IN
ACTIVITIES ENSURING THAT
—A comprehensive program of community
  relations is established.

Case Study 103

The board of education told the new superintendent, Tom Page, that the district needs to establish a full program of community relations. The relationship between the district and the community has deteriorated as a result of a teacher strike, some problems with a principal who was dismissed, and other district concerns that were made public.

Tom knows that he must supervise the establishment of this program, which would include a district public relations program as well as public relations programs at each of the schools, under the direction of the principals. He also strongly feels that this effort should not be confined to the schools sending information to the community, but that it must include getting input back from the community. In other words, a good "community relations" program, to him, is more than just a good "public information" program.

Discussion Questions

1 How would you start this program initially? Who would you meet with? At what stage should the principals be involved? Should board members who felt strongly about this issue be involved in these discussions?

2 Look at the list that follows and decide whether each item should be included in the community relations program and, if so, how it should be included at the district level and at the individual school level:

- publications about what is going on
- an annual report emphasizing financial matters
- press releases to the media on special events or accomplishments
- meetings with organized community groups (e. g., Rotary)
- meetings with other community members
- involvement with the local PTA groups
- one or more parent or community advisory groups
- a formal survey of parents' (or community) opinions about the school
- invitation to people to visit the schools or visit with administrators
- special events at school for special groups (e. g., Thanksgiving lunch at school for a senior citizens organization the day before Thanksgiving, a free musical program)

3 Looking at the list in #2, to whom should the written materials be sent? Who should be selected from the school to attend the meetings? What should they talk about? What survey questions would be helpful to ask? What would you do with people who were invited to the school during the regular school day?

4 What other suggestions would you have to make the community relations program comprehensive and successful?

Comments

Principals and superintendents have to be careful to avoid a program that tells parents/community members everything but does not ask them anything. Parents want to know what is going on in the school, but they also want to have ways to make suggestions. A comparison could be made to a teacher who lectures to the students all the time. The students can learn something, but they would do better if they were allowed to ask questions, make some suggestions, and become involved in the class.

Any publications, as well as regular written notices that are sent to parents, must be examined carefully to see if they are accurate, with correct spelling and acceptable grammar. Some people love to find errors in things sent from schools. To them, such errors prove that the school people do not know how to spell, for example.

Administrators need to meet with the media to see how press releases will be helpful to the media and when they should be written. Also, the professionals in this field can tell the school personnel what type of stories they seek for publication.

When doing a written survey of parents or community members, be sure you know what you are doing—or hire an expert to help you. You need to word questions appropriately, decide whether you are going to send it to everyone or to a random sample, and decide how you will tabulate the results and what you will do with them when you have them, especially if the results are not so complimentary on some aspects of the school. (One of the authors did such a survey and got a very low score on the parents' perception of the board of education members even though scores on the administrative staff were satisfactory. The board did not like these results!)

PERFORMANCE OBJECTIVE

THE ADMINISTRATOR FACILITATES
PROCESSES AND ENGAGES IN
ACTIVITIES ENSURING THAT
—Public resources and funds are used
  appropriately and wisely.

Case Study 104

When the new superintendent arrived in the district, he met with the business manager, John Rogers, to discuss the school's budget. He examined the details of the budget and looked at the actual contracts of the 100 teachers in the district. Later in the week, the superintendent, Dr. Mayer, took the contracts and computed the teacher salaries on an adding machine. Looking at the line item in the budget for teacher salaries, Dr. Mayer noticed that the teacher salary total he got when he added them up was far more than the amount listed in the budget for "teacher salaries."

Dr. Mayer approached Mr. Rogers and asked him about the difference. Mr. Rogers explained, "If I had included all of the teacher salaries in the budget, we would not have had a balanced budget for next year." The superintendent contacted the school board president who said, "Last year we had some financial problems, and we were so happy that John had presented a 'balanced budget' to us this year. I think we had better have an executive session of the board so you can discuss this matter with us. We may have a personnel problem on our hands."

Discussion Questions

1 If you had been Dr. Mayer, would you have done the same thing he did when he found this difference in salaries?

2 Was the fact that Dr. Mayer checked the budget against the salaries evidence that he does not trust other administrators, or was it appropriate for him to do this?

3 When Dr. Mayer meets with the board in executive session, what should he say? What materials, if any, should he take to the meeting? Should he contact the school attorney now or wait until the board

meeting? What should he tell John Rogers about the upcoming board meeting since it must be posted publicly (even though the session will be closed)?

4 Assuming that Dr. Mayer's figures are accurate, what recommendations should the new superintendent make to the board? Is this sufficient cause to dismiss the business manager?

5 If any action is taken against the business manager, how will the school staff and public view the "new guy on the block," Dr. Mayer?

Comments

This case study was a real one, encountered by one of the authors as a new superintendent. The board did meet in closed session and discussed the situation. When other financial problems came to light during the discussion and in the following days, the board president and superintendent met with the school attorney and suspended the business manager. After looking at the whole financial situation, the budget, and the actions of the business manager in other areas, the district fired the business manager after holding an appropriate hearing in private. The superintendent assumed the duties of the business manager for the remainder of his years in the district. The next superintendent hired an assistant superintendent for business.

PERFORMANCE OBJECTIVE

THE ADMINISTRATOR FACILITATES
PROCESSES AND ENGAGES IN
ACTIVITIES ENSURING THAT
—Public resources and funds are used
  appropriately and wisely.

Case Study 105

Sometimes a district can have financial problems that involve small amounts of money but have the potential for big headlines. Here is another case that actually happened.

Two of the high school teachers, Jim and Ralph, volunteered to supervise all of the school dances held after home football games and basketball games. Their procedure was to collect an admission price at the door and keep the money in a box. If the students felt they needed a newly released record or CD for the dance, Jim would give a student some money to go purchase it. At the close of the evening, Jim and Ralph would take what they thought was appropriate for their pay from the money in the box. As Ralph said, "Some nights we did better than others."

Discussion Questions

1 As the high school principal, what do you think of this procedure? Do you see any problems?

2 If you want to change the procedure, what would you do?

3 How would you deal with Jim and Ralph who have volunteered to supervise these dances when others could not be bothered?

Comments

As stated earlier, this case study did happen. Jim and Ralph were told that, in the future, they would be paid a set amount (negotiated with the union, if necessary), and would be paid the same amount each dance regardless of the number of students attending (and the amount collected). Both Jim and Ralph refused to supervise under these conditions, which tells us something about the past practice of taking what they wanted from the box. Since other teachers did not want the supervision, the principal said that school organizations could sponsor the dances, with their faculty sponsors, and that all the money collected would go to the sponsoring organizations. This seemed to work well.

PERFORMANCE OBJECTIVE

THE ADMINISTRATOR FACILITATES
PROCESSES AND ENGAGES IN
ACTIVITIES ENSURING THAT
—Community collaboration is modeled for
  staff.

Case Study 106

The superintendent and board of education invited the school principals and a representative group of teachers to attend a meeting they held with community personnel. The board hoped that these guests would see what it, along with the superintendent, was trying to accomplish to promote collaboration with the community at the board/superintendent level. This particular school district covered territory that included seven different communities. The board invited the mayor of each town for a buffet supper and conversation with the board and the central administration. After the meal, everyone adjourned to a large room in one of the schools where each board member and central administrator explained one facet of the district's goals. These ranged from financial to curriculum to construction to public policy. The board president encouraged the mayors to discuss these topics and to contribute their views and ideas. As the meeting progressed, certain mayors agreed to meet on a regular basis with the presenter of a particular topic to discuss it further and to find ways for the district and the communities to work together on that topic.

Discussion Questions

1 What do you think about this district-community meeting? Was it a good idea or just a PR effort?
2 Is this a good example of a collaborative project that could serve as a model for district staff? What are some other examples you can think of or ones you have experienced?
3 Is it important to have community collaboration at all? If so, why is it important?
4 What is the difference among (1) community collaboration, (2) public relations efforts, and (3) sending people to speak to community groups?
5 Note that the board president ran the meeting rather than the superintendent. Who would you choose from these two? Why? What are the advantages/disadvantages of each running the meeting?
6 The principal/teacher guests were supposed to merely observe the meeting. Was this appropriate?

7 Who should benefit from any collaboration—the district or the community?

PERFORMANCE OBJECTIVE

THE ADMINISTRATOR FACILITATES
PROCESSES AND ENGAGES IN
ACTIVITIES ENSURING THAT
—Opportunities for staff to develop
  collaborative skills are provided.

Case Study 107

At the scheduled monthly faculty meeting, the principal asks participants, all of whom have gathered in the library at work tables, to remain with the group they are seated with throughout the upcoming series of monthly meetings. The principal then suggests a brief 10-minute dialogue about "collaboration" and urges each group to evolve a working definition of the term. Groups are to take notes about ideas offered and retain all notes for the remainder of the group's work.

After group dialogue and the working definitions, the groups use the next 10 minutes to focus on refining "effective collaborative skills." Each group then shares ideas with the larger group. A list of the collaborative skills is written on an easel pad at the front of the room. Copies of all ideas will be given to all participants. Then, additional time is spent discussing ideas about involving more parent/guardians and community members, as well as personnel connected with community organizations and other resources outside the school setting. Again, individual group ideas are shared with the group at large.

In two days, all participants involved receive information in their office mailboxes detailing the definition of "collaboration," a list of collaborative skills necessary in successful group efforts, and 26 separate ideas about involving more stakeholders in the district's educational program.

At the subsequent faculty meeting, faculty members resume their places with the groups they met with in the library. Groups generate a list of community resources and organizations they feel are important adjuncts to the learning situation. Then they list student and school problems that need attention. As a side note, in this district, interestingly enough, four of the five groups cite student attitude problems. Specifically, students' materialism and isolation from "the real world" are listed as serious shortcomings. This is thought to be, in part, a result of the school's location in an affluent Chicago North Shore area.

The final exercise involves pairing perceived problems and concerns with community resources and organizations. Each committee elects teams of two members to consult and collaborate with their targeted "useful resources"; the goal is to establish school-community partnerships, even for a limited time, to address specific concerns. But first, all groups meet and share their concerns with the larger group in order to avoid duplication of efforts.

Discussion Questions

1 Is the approach described above useful? Workable? How else might collaborative skills be learned and practiced? For example, some districts hire consultants for inservice days or stage retreats away from school.

2 Predict the use of the technique described above in your own district, with your faculty. What factors might inhibit success? Does each group need a chairman or leader, as well as note-taker?

3 At some point, might instructors have turned to district administrators, including the superintendent, for input about their concerns? If you agree, at what point is this advisable?

4 Is the use of the technique described above putting ("as usual," some might argue) all of the responsibility on already overburdened faculty members? Is it better to give teachers a choice about participation or not?

5 The "train the teacher" model described takes a lot of time. Might the end justify the time commitment? What types of problems stand a chance of being solved using this method of outreach? What specific problems related to students and the school might *not* be managed or solved in using this kind of strategy?

6 What introductory remarks would a school leader be wise to include in explaining this strategy when the first faculty meeting occurs, before the initial dialogue exercise begins?

7 How much authority and leeway should faculty members be given in carrying out their inquiries with representatives of community resources and organizations? What kinds of things necessitate approval from administrators or board authorization?

CHAPTER 7

Standard 5 Case Studies

A school administrator is an educational leader who promotes the success of all students by acting with integrity, fairness, and in an ethical manner.

PERFORMANCE OBJECTIVE

THE ADMINISTRATOR
—examines personal and professional values, demonstrates a personal and professional code of ethics, and serves as a role model

Case Study 108

Consider the following examples:

- The brilliant head of Computer Technology routinely makes jokes about the economic status and perceived "desirability" of other communities as he gives his yearly presentation to the faculty about scheduling and computer complexities. True, this district is affluent and well known; everyone feels fortunate to be part of the school system. One example of his jokes: "You know they're a bunch of hicks in beautiful downtown Center Prairie." People laugh, since it is a joke.
- An attractive teacher new to the district invites senior students (male and female) to her mobile home after school—to socialize with and to counsel students. She disagrees with some of the counselors' suggestions for the students' college and career plans, for example.

- The principal warns teachers not to fail athletes or the children of important community leaders unless there is "a long paper trail, from Day 1, of course." As he says, "We have a responsibility in this town, and we need all the good folks' support out there."

- Another principal uses verbal intimidation and threats of job loss ("Do that again, and I'll personally see to it that you are not rehired!") to maintain control of her faculty. She likes things done a certain way—or else. She encourages teachers she likes to "keep an eye on" those teachers she doesn't like and offers a variety of desirable perks as rewards.

- The district's policy is not to issue pay checks until after 4 : 00 P.M. on pay days (when local banks are closed), or on "the next working day" if pay day falls on Friday. The superintendent himself distributes the checks to each faculty member as they line up in his office; checks are issued after school has dismissed for the day. He says things aloud, such as: "You certainly don't deserve this" or "I know you really didn't earn your money this month." Unfortunately, he is not joking. Teachers have put up with these comments for years

- The principal encourages an administrative intern to schedule a job interview in another district and tells her to apply for a personal leave day as soon as possible. When the intern leaves the office to apply for the day's absence, she stops to fill out a "Request for Absence" form and inadvertently overhears the principal call the superintendent, telling him not to approve a paid leave day because it involves seeking another job. "We'll have to pay a substitute—Eileen [the intern] should be grateful to have a job in our district, don't you think so, Ed?" Ed agrees and refuses the request.

- A superintendent listens to a sales representative's recital that includes hints of "special bonuses" available—actually, kickbacks—in accepting his company's bids for contracts with the district. The superintendent is not accepting the offers but shows interest in order to gauge how far the sales representative will go to get a sale.

Discussion Questions

1 Respond to the ethical norms involved in each real-life scenario described above.

2 Is there one set of ethical standards applying to all adult members of a school community? Should such a document exist? How does one create a document of this nature? Recall the Rotarian Four-Way Test, including such questions as "Is it fair to all?"

3 How should administrators, faculty, and staff reveal to students the ethical imperatives that govern many businesses in this country? Note: Many of these have their own codes that potential employees must agree to.

4 "Administrators and faculty are trained professionals who do not need stated ethical norms," insists one member of the school community. Is this true? Does one's license or endorsement guarantee that one will act ethically and professionally at all times?

Comments

The strength of a district, as well as its reputation, rests with the conduct and proprieties of its administrators and staff members. An ethical code of conduct, written or unwritten, requires compliance. However, administrators, faculty, and staff members must know that these standards exist. Administrators have an obligation to explain their high expectations for appropriate, ethical handling of all matters by its faculty and staff, whether they are on or off campus.

PERFORMANCE OBJECTIVE
THE ADMINISTRATOR
—examines personal and professional
values, demonstrates a personal and
professional code of ethics, and serves as
a role model

Case Study 109

John Gardner, a superintendent in a suburban district, was reading his state's *School Board Journal* and noticed an article urging boards to adopt a Code of Ethics that had been prepared by the American School Boards Association. The *Journal* had a copy of the code printed in the article he was reading. That seemed like a good idea. At times his board seemed to wonder what was proper to do, and he noticed that the code addressed some areas that the board had discussed.

At the next board meeting the superintendent said to the board, "In your board packet I sent you a copy of the Code of Ethics for school board members, which has been prepared by your national association. I read in the state's *Journal* that boards should adopt this code to help guide them in their actions. I think it is a good idea, and that is why I sent you the code and the article in your packet."

One recently elected board member responded, "I don't think it is necessary for us to adopt any code. We know what we want to do and how we want to do things here. We don't need any national code to guide us." Another member gave a weak response, saying that the code sounded OK to her. No one else said anything, and the board took no action.

Discussion Questions

1 Should Mr. Gardner have pursued the matter more at this board meeting, perhaps asking for other opinions?

2 Should Mr. Gardner have made a stronger pitch for the adoption of the code?

3 What should the board president have done?

4 Should the superintendent drop this idea completely? If not, how should he pursue it in the future?

5 What does the first board member's response tell you about him? Do you think he is just against some code sent from a national body or is it something else?

6 What about the lack of response of the board as a whole? Should the superintendent really be concerned about a board that will not adopt a Code of Ethics written by its own national organization, or is this some power struggle having nothing to do with ethics?

PERFORMANCE OBJECTIVE

THE ADMINISTRATOR
—examines personal and professional
values, demonstrates a personal and
professional code of ethics, and serves as
a role model

Case Study 110

Dr. Harvey, the superintendent, received a phone call from one of the board members, Joan Peterson. "Dr. Harvey, I just found out something and feel we have to do something as a board—or maybe you have to do something—but I don't know what. Remember last night in executive session, we discussed negotiations and talked about how much salary we might give the teachers and how we wanted to word some of their language proposals? Well, it seems that after the meeting, Tom [another board member] went to a pizza place and met with the head negotiator for the teachers! I doubt if they were just discussing what kind of pizza to order. What should we do? Can we keep Tom out of executive sessions or what?"

Discussion Questions

1 What should Dr. Harvey say to Joan?

2 What steps should the superintendent take? What should the board do?

3 Assuming that Tom did meet with the head negotiator, should he be confronted about this? If so, who should do it?

4 Assuming that Tom did, in fact, discuss the board strategy with the teachers, what should the board do about it?

5 What if the rest of the board feels that it is a violation of confidentiality and ethics to talk to others about executive session business, but Tom feels that all board discussions should be shared with others?

Comments

Different states have different laws about open and closed meetings, and some states require only open meetings. The state where the above occurred allows closed sessions to discuss collective bargaining positions (among other topics), and board members are not supposed to discuss the contents of those meetings outside of the session. Also, that state makes no provision for the exclusion of any board member from board meetings because of such action that Tom took. The board should probably confront Tom in an executive session and let him know their feelings. The president of the board, or some other member, should speak to him at this session, or privately, rather than have the superintendent do it. It is not good for the superintendent's future to have to be the one to confront board members about ethical problems. If Tom persists, the board may have to avoid discussion of collective bargaining at meetings and trust in the superintendent or negotiator to bargain an appropriate contract. The superintendent can always call the board president on the phone to discuss specifics on the progress in negotiations.

PERFORMANCE OBJECTIVE

THE ADMINISTRATOR
—demonstrates values, beliefs, and attitudes
  that inspire others to higher levels of
  performance

Case Study 111

Principal Ray Anderson respects and values each individual he meets. He listens to people and seems interested in what they say. Modest and unassuming, Ray takes his job very seriously, but he is a behind-the-scenes leader. He relies on his 20-year background in education, mostly as an administrator. As a principal, he is rarely noticed; you may have to catch him in the hall because that's usually where he is—there or somewhere in the building trouble-shooting problems.

Russ Peterson, on the other hand, resembles a football linebacker rather than a principal. Students routinely grab his arms and challenge him to wrestling contests in the hallways. It is his enthusiasm that affects faculty and staff members. He loves young adults, the district, and his job. He seems to enjoy coming to work every day. Peterson can solve any problem with his pragmatic, common-sense approach to things.

A third principal is R.J. Horner, a meticulous detail man in control of "his" school. He spends almost all of his time visible in the building, tape recorder in hand, noting repairs necessary, unlocked doors, broken windows, and other maintenance tasks. He wants to monitor the building during the entire school day, as he believes that a well-run facility with everything working will encourage carry-over into the classroom. He dislikes paperwork, reports, and any kind of record-keeping and delegates all of that to others.

Discussion Questions

1 What values, beliefs, and attitudes might the three principals described model for their faculties and staffs?

2 What specific values, beliefs, and attitudes are common to principals who inspire others to high levels of performance? Conversely, what values, beliefs, and attitudes interfere with a principal's success on the job and his/her ability to inspire others?

3 Describe school administrators, including superintendents, who have inspired you or continue to inspire you to high levels of performance. What particular qualities did each possess?

Comments

It is vital that faculty and staff members hold school administrators in high esteem. A job in education is too difficult otherwise, and the day-by-day challenges might be overwhelming. On the other hand, effective administrative styles do not simply emerge. It would seem that seasoned administrators with years of experience become effective at their jobs because of their wide range of experiences. Nothing surprises them. Is this true? Can graduate schools simply warn potential administrators "Be yourself and work hard in order to succeed"? What inspires outstanding dedication and performance among faculty and staff members? What values, beliefs, and attitudes must administrators model? How do they acquire these if they do not occur naturally as a part of one's personality?

PERFORMANCE OBJECTIVE

THE ADMINISTRATOR
—accepts responsibility for school operations

Case Study 112

Mr. Barber had just returned from an administrative meeting downtown when his secretary, Mrs. Squires, appeared at his office door. "Yes, Mrs. Squires?" He could tell that something was wrong by the secretary's demeanor.

"Mr. Barber," she began in a very serious tone. "There is a man in our outer office who is bleeding and complaining about a hurt back. He says he hit an overhanging branch that is on our school property and was knocked to the ground. He is bleeding somewhat profusely and has caused quite a stir in the outer office."

The tree in question was well known to Mr. Barber. Just last week while on a tour of the grounds, he noticed the branches were both low and overhanging to the point that they impeded pedestrians on the sidewalk. In fact, he had told Mr. Sorensen, the custodian, to cut down the branches before someone walked into them and got hurt.

He immediately rose from his seat and followed Mrs. Squires to the outer office where he encountered an elderly gentleman with a blood-soaked handkerchief on his forehead. Mr. Barber swallowed hard and tried to remember exactly what he had said to Mr. Sorensen about the tree. He also tried to remember the date of their conversation as he approached the gentleman and began expressing concern for his health and safety. "I am so sorry that this accident occurred," Mr. Barber said in a low voice, trying to mask both his anger at Mr. Sorensen and his surprise at what had just occurred. "Are you all right? Is there anything we can do, or anyone we can call? Do you live around here?"

It was obvious the man was in terrible pain as he gingerly moved to stand up. "My name is Adams, and I live in this neighborhood. As to a call, I would say *yes,* call my lawyer because I am going to sue you and the district for as much as I can. There is no excuse for a public institution to allow trees to grow in such a manner that they might injure pedestrians walking and minding their own business.''

"I understand your anger, Mr. Adams. Let us get you cleaned up and perhaps we should call the paramedics to check you out. Then we can discuss your accident.''

After the paramedics took Mr. Adams to the emergency room, Mr. Barber contacted the superintendent and the school district attorney. Both asked him the same two questions: "How badly was Mr. Adams hurt?'' and "Do you have a copy of the memorandum directing the custodian to trim the trees?''

Mr. Barber explained that he had not given Mr. Sorensen a *written* memorandum. He said that he had verbally directed Mr. Sorensen to trim the trees on the school grounds. Mr. Barber knew of the problem, but he told the superintendent he was willing to assume all responsibility for Mr. Sorensen's inaction since he was the principal of the building. He told the superintendent that the problem would be remedied immediately and he would go to the hospital or to Mr. Adams's home to try and reason with him.

Discussion Questions

1 What is the principal's responsibility when it comes to the operation of the school building and grounds?

2 Was Mr. Barber remiss for not giving Mr. Sorensen a written memorandum directing him to cut and trim the trees on the premises?

3 Could the secretary, Mrs. Squires, have mitigated the situation by being more solicitous and concerned about Mr. Adams?

4 How would you have handled Mr. Adams after you found that he had been involved in the accident?

5 Was Mr. Barber correct in immediately contacting the superintendent?

6 Was Mr. Barber correct in immediately contacting the school district attorney?

7 What do you feel would be the liability of the district?

8 Do you believe that Mr. Barber should allow himself to be blamed for this accident?

9 If you were the principal, what would you do about Mr. Sorensen?

PERFORMANCE OBJECTIVE

THE ADMINISTRATOR
—considers the impact of one's
administrative practices on others

Case Study 113

Alice Greenleaf had been excited about her first principalship. While some things probably went quite well, she had a feeling that others did not, but she did not know why. She spent quite a bit of time thinking about what she had done, and she still could not understand why there seemed to be some negative feelings about her. Maybe she just imagined it all!

Alice started Monday by sending individual teachers memos that she had written to them over the weekend. She always reserved part of Sunday afternoon so that she could think about the school and what needed to be done. Then she wrote the memos so that they could be in mailboxes Monday morning. She prided herself on her efficiency, and this was just one example. (She had talked to a fellow principal who said that he never wrote memos but visited teachers when he wanted to tell them something. You could spend a whole day just doing that, Alice thought.)

At Tuesday's teacher meeting, Alice was taken by surprise when Janet asked whether they were going to get the computers "in my lifetime." Alice explained to Janet that although she had promised that each teacher would have a computer connected to the district office and to the Internet, she later found that no funds were available. It was not her fault.

On Wednesday, two teachers came up to Alice and asked why the process on book selection had been changed for the next year. Alice patiently told them that a principal had to make a lot of tough decisions in a short period of time and that she had not had time to explain to the staff all the reasons behind every decision. This decision was one that she had to make quickly.

Thursday at the Principal's Advisory Committee, Alice stated that she had set the date for the Open House, had established committees, arranged a timetable, and made decisions as to what activities would be a part of the Open House. However, she wanted to share her decision-making with the committee by having them decide on what food should be served and who should be asked to bring each food item.

Friday afternoon, Alice met with the superintendent who wanted to check to see how she was doing. Alice said, "I think things are going great. The school seems to be running well, and I am working on Open House now."

The superintendent paused and then said, "Alice, sometimes we do not realize that what we do as administrators has an impact on our teachers. Do you think about your impact on your teachers?"

Discussion Questions

1 Alice probably did not understand the superintendent's point. Maybe you can help her. Looking at Monday, what impact could there be of sending memos to teachers instead of talking to them personally?

2 On Tuesday, the subject of computers came up. What happens when an administrator promises something to teachers and cannot follow through? Can you think of examples where an administrator did something just like this? How did the teachers (or others) feel? Were there any long-term feelings towards this administrator?

3 What's the big deal about explaining administrative decisions to teachers in Wednesday's example? Aren't administrators paid to make decisions—isn't that enough, without having to explain "why, why, why" all the time?

4 On Thursday, Alice wanted to share decision-making with the teachers on the Advisory Committee. Do you see the problem here?

Comments

This author was once told, "The teachers want to know who made the decision and why." It seemed that the source of the decision-making was more important that what the decision was. Administrators must remember that teachers (and other administrators) *do* want to know who makes the decisions and why they are made. Many problems would be avoided if the decision-maker would initially tell the teachers why the decision had to be made and why other approaches could not be taken. Also, teachers usually want to be a part of the decision-making process, but they do not want to be stuck with unimportant decisions. It is a waste of their time. The things that administrators do, whether promising something and not delivering or sending impersonal memos, have an impact on the others in the building or district.

PERFORMANCE OBJECTIVE

THE ADMINISTRATOR
—uses the influence of the office to enhance the educational program rather than for personal gain

Case Study 114

Consider the priorities of these three school administrators.

1 The superintendent of District 209 is justifiably proud of his position; his high school is often cited as "one of the best in the country." He is careful about the school's reputation, so when district students recently did less well than expected on the standardized tests, he altered score reports slightly. Justifying this with the realization that the tests are never perfect, or test the real abilities of students, he wants to "make everyone happy." As he views it, planning for the future: "We have got to make those teachers teach to the tests, like everyone else does."

2 A gifted administrator, the new district curriculum coordinator has far-reaching powers. However, though she enjoys working in the district, she has to look out for her own future. She wants a plum job at the state university and knows it will be available in a year or two. Her reputation is at stake, and she needs to call attention to her work now. Accordingly, she plans a total revision of all courses and programs; she will mandate all new goals and objectives, in line with state recommendations. How else, she wonders, can she make a name for herself in so short a time? Besides, she

is sure the curriculum needs reworking: most curricula can use revision.

3 "I'm looking out for myself," one superintendent tells a friend when they meet at the national convention. "My contract was not renewed in my last district, and I put my whole family in jeopardy. Never again! I intend to be the 'yes man' in this district. Anything that the board wants to do is O.K. by me. The same applies to administrators and teachers. This will be one smooth-running, happy place. I am going to please everyone. I just finished the Dale Carnegie course, you know. It will look like we are the best school district in this state, and I know they will renew my contract again and again. This is a game, and you have to know how to play it; it's a prevent defense all the way."

Discussion Questions

1 How may the educational program suffer at the hands of the administrators described above? On the other hand, don't you need a "healthy selfishness" as an administrator? Shouldn't you try to make a good impression?

2 Times are tough, and good positions in good districts are hard to come by. Once you get a top position, shouldn't you play it smart and safe and do everything you can (whatever it takes, actually) to keep the job? Isn't that the bottom line?

3 What is the best balance of making good decisions that allow for personal self-interest and commitment to the educational program of the district? What rules should govern one's conduct and decisions? How do you know when you are "on target" with that balance between your own needs and the demands of the district?

Comments

Let's assume the position of a devil's advocate.

School administrators have earned the right to protect themselves and take whatever steps are necessary to guarantee their job security and that next position. It is just being realistic, if not smart. Effective school leaders have to have a healthy selfishness and look out for themselves. Education isn't a game in which everyone wins. You must build your own reputation with a series of successes, however you can do it. Who else is going to look out for you and your welfare, if not your family? Sadly enough, most administrators have seen firsthand proof of the fact that the "good guys" rarely win.

PERFORMANCE OBJECTIVE

THE ADMINISTRATOR
—uses the influence of the office to enhance the educational program rather than for personal gain

Case Study 115

Robert Harris, a superintendent in a medium-size town, was talking to a retired superintendent one evening. As might be expected, talk led to a discussion about schools and their boards. Bob said, "Jim, I always have felt that principals, superintendents, and school board members should have the education of the students as their first priority rather than be looking at what they can get out of it for themselves."

"Well, I can't disagree with that. Sure, we make a living from the job, and school board members get some publicity, which some seek, but I agree that we have to concentrate on the students. What's your point, Bob?"

"It's the board. It seems that they keep coming up with things they want to have done for themselves instead of for the kids. I hardly know what to do—tell them to get their priorities straight and maybe lose my job or just go along with their petty requests."

"What are these petty requests?" Jim asked.

"Where do I start?" Bob responded. "Let me name a few. One board member stated that he wanted business cards printed for each board member. I sure don't know who would ever ask them for any, but I checked and found we could print them fairly cheaply here at school. When I told them that, the same guy said that he wanted the cards to be *embossed,* not just printed, and he wanted different colors on the cards."

"That seems a waste of money, Bob. What else did they want?"

"Well, they stated that they wanted display boards placed in every school building with their names and titles on them—only two have titles, of course, the president and the secretary of the board. We did it, against my better judgment. And, wait until you hear this one, Jim! I was mowing the yard one evening, and my wife called me in to take a phone call from a board member, Barbara Ray. Barbara called to tell me that she had visited one of the buildings that day and her name had no title next to it. And this is the best part. The board only voted her vice president last night, yet she expected all these signs to be changed overnight, it appears."

"But, Bob, we don't have vice presidents of boards in this state."

"I know. That's what I mean. She wanted an office so badly that she convinced that board that they should have a vice president just in case the president can't make it some night." So they elected her to an office that does not even exist! I could give you other examples, but this gives you an idea of what I mean. Any suggestions?"

Discussion Questions

1 What advice can Jim give the superintendent?

2 What motivates board members to act like this?

3 Can anything be done to make board members like these feel more important so that they will not use their office for personal gain? For example, can they be appointed to special committees or sent to state board meetings as representatives of the whole board?

4 What should Bob do when board members make requests like these at public board meetings?

5 Does this case study say something about why board members are elected? About what type of people are sometimes elected? Years ago the elected (or appointed) board members were leading citizens of the town, the bankers, doctors, etc. Is this true today? If not, why not?

PERFORMANCE OBJECTIVE

THE ADMINISTRATOR
—treats people fairly, equitably, and with
  dignity and respect

Case Study 116

In the view of A. Cortez, the close of the school year was welcome; she would remember it as a demanding but rewarding year. Appointed interim principal by the city board, her challenge had been clearly mandated by board members: Make Cityview High School more like the school it was 20 years ago. The board specified a review of curriculum, a revised disciplinary code, and a businesslike school climate where educational efforts were accorded top priority. Cortez had worked to achieve those goals, and she was satisfied she had made significant strides with students and staff.

Reading the evaluations of the professional staff, however, caused Cortez some alarm. She was perceived as ''one who favors certain groups.'' Other comments written by hand were also startlingly unfavorable: ''Cortez criticizes professionals unfairly and overwhelms them''; ''Does not always treat teachers well, is demanding''; ''The principal needs to respect the hard-working teachers''; and ''I felt demoralized at some of our faculty meetings.''

At first angered that fellow professionals did not realize how much effort she had expended to stabilize Cityview High School, Cortez realized she might have overlooked opportunities to establish good relationships with her most valued asset, the professional staff. Cortez reviewed her options for the summer session ahead and the fall term, resolving to change things. She created a list of ideas:

- Model professionalism (make a list of the key traits a professional educator should exhibit and keep a copy in the office where I can see it at all times).
- Get into the teachers' lounge, offices, and workroom on a regular basis; welcome teachers' concerns and conversation.
- Greet all faculty and staff as enthusiastically as I do students.
- Create an ''open office door'' policy as well as more free time to meet with teachers and support staff; maintain accessibility.
- Bring in breakfast pastries or breads once a month.
- Send ''Good News'' notes every week: Pick a department and ''catch'' teachers doing things well (being on time for duty assignments, being in the hall between classes, turning in reports on schedule); follow up with verbal praise.

- Single out the unique approaches of various departments as they work with the new curriculum to engage students in learning.
- Create time at the beginning of faculty meetings to listen to teachers' concerns—and follow up on these as needed.
- Apologize for being less than sensitive and explain the priorities and goals of the city board; seek input, suggestions, at first faculty meeting.
- Make sure to apply handbook "rules" with scrupulous fairness as situations arise.
- Smile more; exchange positive impressions with professional staff as they occur.
- Allow faculty members to express their suggestions for more efficient school operations; increase their autonomy wherever possible.
- Treat every individual in the school community as I would like to be treated.
- Start each faculty meeting with a review of how much I value the hard work and commitment of staff members; thank faculty and encourage their efforts; be specific with praise.

Discussion Questions

1 How can Cortez guarantee that she will apply handbook rules with "scrupulous fairness" in the future? Can you advise her about safeguarding the fair and equitable treatment of all members of the school community?

2 Is a busy principal also expected to become a public relations specialist, in addition to all the other job demands? Note: Some administrators are more open, warm, and caring than others, but others might be top-notch professionals with gifts that "count" more than personality traits that please their staffs.

3 What is a *professional* administrator in an educational setting? Can you provide a working definition, however brief? What traits, attitudes, and behaviors reveal educational professionalism? A list might include "Observes discretion and confidentiality on sensitive subjects" or "Acts in an honest, ethical, and forthright manner."

4 Will Cortez's resolve to "smile more" and bring in pastries make a difference? More importantly, should an administrator ever apologize for doing the job as that administrator perceives it needs to be done?

5 What guidelines would you give an administrator new to the job in terms of treating people "with dignity and respect"? What shows those two qualities? How does one acquire and display them?

6 Describe an administrator you know who displays the ideal, "Treats people fairly, equitably, and with dignity and respect." How would that administrator view Cortez's dismay at the evaluative comments and her list of notes and suggestions?

Comments

One cannot simply legislate an administrator's personality and style. School settings demand that administrators, faculty, and staff work hard to understand each other's point of view, responsibilities, and priorities—especially in these demanding times and challenging work settings. Cortez seems to have taken some negative comments very much to heart; perhaps these observations come from staff members who preferred the previous administrator. These negative voices may even represent the cadre of pessimists who sometimes remain in school settings they dislike, in a profession they feel has failed them. One must be careful about balancing input on evaluations. If a professional staff chooses not to see the progress this administrator has made, it seems that the fault is theirs. If she has success in making an impact in her first year at Cityview High, she probably is a talented, committed administrator.

PERFORMANCE OBJECTIVE

THE ADMINISTRATOR
—protects the rights and confidentiality of
   students and staff

Case Study 117

A principal with strong views and a proprietary interest in everything that impacts the students and staff in one building feels that a faculty is similar to soldiers new to the armed services. Both need molding, strict discipline, a no-nonsense approach to education, and an emphasis on doing all things in a prescribed and timely manner.

Recently, a teacher described problems with one particular student, confiding to another teacher details about the parent, Mrs. Salman, who is "extremely overprotective" of her son. The two of them were the only ones to share third-hour prep period in the lounge that day, and the teacher who asked for input has no doubt that the request for strict confidentiality about their conversation will be honored.

Imagine the surprise when the principal calls the teacher into the office within days of the conversation and mentions extremely specific details and exact quotes from the supposedly private conversation about young Salman. Having questioned the longtime teaching associate/ friend, there is no doubt that the principal listened to their conversation. In fact, rumors in the building suggest that the administrator switches on the intercom at will, wherever desired, in order to keep abreast of everything going on in the school. The rationale? It is a principal's right and responsibility to monitor the building. Word has gotten around school about the seemingly overheard conversation in the lounge.

Discussion Questions

1 Varying styles of leadership allow administrators a rather wide berth in running the kind of district/school that produces results in terms of student learning. At what point, however, does a style of leadership interfere with teachers doing their jobs and the education of young people?

2 Under what circumstances does an administrator have the right/ duty to monitor the conversations of faculty and staff members? What does an administrator do about rumors he/she overhears?

3 Some administrators routinely use "stooges" to find out whatever they need to know, to anticipate problems within the building, and to know what various staff members are up to. Let's face it, union members employ somewhat questionable tactics; it's just common sense to get a jump on them. In exchange for information, administrators may give some teachers "a break" when they need it (preferential scheduling of classes, for example). It all evens out, doesn't

it? The education of young people is at stake, as well as the effective operation of the school. What is your opinion?

4 What specific steps can this and other administrators take to show teachers the dedication, interest, and commitment that they have to their staff and students?

Comments

Teachers respond favorably to administrators who treat them as adults, believe in their abilities, and trust their good judgment. Everyone makes mistakes; the important thing is how we respond to our problems and what we learn from them. Administrators who take the time to visit classes, respond to teachers' concerns, give very specific praise for particularly effective professional service, and view each problem as a challenge with a potential for an effective outcome are respected as committed educators. Principals must be effective problem-solvers who are visible or accessible a majority of the school day. Modeling good communication skills and believing wholeheartedly in students, faculty, and staff is a good start. What should principals do to establish good relationships with their faculty and staff members?

PERFORMANCE OBJECTIVE

THE ADMINISTRATOR
—demonstrates appreciation for and
  sensitivity to the diversity in the school
  community

Case Study 118

Two school administrators converse at a local conference:

"My district really reflects the global marketplace now that International UOP set up headquarters at the edge of town. Have you seen that place? It's almost a city unto itself; they have built a huge indoor pool and a bowling alley for employees!"

"I know! Your district will be in good financial shape for years to come. And about the diversity thing—it's the same in my district. Oh, we're still an 'exclusive suburb' kind of school, but it's a world of difference from even two years ago.''

"What are you recommending to the board about holidays and all the cultural celebrations? There are so many cultural groups represented at school. I don't want to offend or slight anyone, but I'm not usually in favor of interrupting school programs for that kind of thing.''

"Well, don't you feel an obligation to recognize all the groups? You might want to call on diversity scholars and see what they think. We've got a consul's son in our school, so I am even more attuned to the topic. I think we are obligated with so many different ethnic and cultural groups represented in the student body. Customs are different everywhere, and most groups fiercely value their own identity and cultural history. They expect recognition, as I see it.''

Discussion Questions

1 Is it a good idea to single out different cultural groups for recognition and encourage all others to know them, their countries, histories, and traditions? Or is it better to keep the amalgam as it is? In other words, allow all members of the school community to assimilate and be equal in the academic setting.

2 What kinds of awareness programs might be necessary for school faculty, staff, and students? Why is this something to consider?

3 Does the school mission statement need revising to reflect its changing populace? How about the course content and programming? History courses? What about school district newsletters? Should articles review the changing populace and encourage awareness and understanding?

4 How aggressive should personnel offices be in hiring administrators, faculty, and staff members to mirror the different ethnic and cultural groups represented in the student body?

Comments

Does "mandated" awareness of and sensitivity to multicultural/multiethnic/multilingual groups work? Students face a global marketplace when they enter the working world, but is it the school's job to teach yet another "special" topic when curricula are already over-loaded? Some parents are notorious for their criticisms of "nonaca-demic" subjects that schools devote attention to. On the other hand, if schools do not assume this responsibility, who will? Do most people simply adapt to working with or living near others who are different, when the need arises?

PERFORMANCE OBJECTIVE

THE ADMINISTRATOR
—recognizes and respects the legitimate
  authority of others

Case Study 119

The new superintendent, Shirley Knott, came out of the last board meeting rather discouraged. She called up her old college professor, Dr. Benedict, and asked him for advice. "Last night, I made some recommendations to the board and they turned them down. I had worked a long time on them and had good arguments as to why they should be approved. The board said that the ideas were good but might not be appropriate for this community. Then they voted them down."

"Well, Shirley, these things happen. You are the new person in town, you know, and these folks have been here for a long time. I hate to say it, but if they really felt that your ideas were not right for them, they probably aren't."

"But, what's the use of even having a superintendent if the board doesn't take my ideas?"

"Shirley, I'm sure they will take most of them. But it is not uncommon for a board to take a different view from the superintendent, even when they all get along very well and agree on most things. You have to realize that, while you may be the professional at the table, the board members still have legitimate reasons to state their opinions and sometimes vote against what you have proposed—or modify it in some way. You have to learn to respect their authority, even though you will not agree with all of their decisions. Remember that you said that you were making some 'recommendations' to them."

Discussion Questions

1 What do you think about Dr. Benedict's response to Shirley?

2 If you were Shirley, would you talk to the board about their relationship and decision-making or just learn from this incident and not mention it at all?

3 If you said you would discuss it with the board, would you do it in a public session or use an executive session (if allowed in your state), or talk to board members on the phone or tell the president to discuss it with the board?

4 If you were a superintendent, like Shirley, how would you cope with the reality of the board turning down your recommendations while still backing you strongly on other things?

5 What are some ways in which Shirley could prepare the board for her recommendations prior to the board meeting where they are being presented to the board?

Comments

Another idea for a superintendent and board to try together is to hold a discussion on the typical types of decisions that they must make during a year: closing a school because of weather problems, hiring a secretary, purchasing paper for the schools, etc. Once a list is made of these decisions, the board and superintendent should discuss who has the authority for decision-making on each item. For example, on some items, the board may say that the superintendent should make the decision and not even bother the board about it. A second response could be for the superintendent to make a decision and inform the board. A third could require that the superintendent bring the decision to the board to make, possibly with a recommendation from the superintendent. Finally, the board may say that it will make the decision alone.

Can you think of other good decisions to discuss? Can you name at least one decision that would fit into each category just named? If the board and the superintendent disagree about who should make the decision in one of these cases, what should be done?

PERFORMANCE OBJECTIVE

THE ADMINISTRATOR
—recognizes and respects the legitimate
authority of others

Case Study 120

The elementary principal, Juan Hernandez, was working on the assignment of students to the third-grade teachers in his building during the summer. On his desk were a bunch of letters from parents requesting (to say the least) that their children be placed in one class or another. Also, his secretary had just left three messages from parents who called with similar requests.

Mr. Hernandez felt that he was the principal and that he should decide which students should be placed in which classes. He never had a choice of teachers when he went to school. On the other hand, he had just attended an area principals' meeting where two principals had given a different view. Both stated that parents who wished a particular teacher should get that teacher, assuming there was room in the class. They stated that they had found that parents who chose the teacher rarely complained later about that teacher, probably because they had made the choice. Also, the parents always seemed to feel that their children were doing well in class.

However, the principals said that the real reason they allowed this choice of teacher was that they felt that they should respect the opinion and choice of the parent—that no one knew what was best for the child any more than the parent. Juan threw the phone messages down on his desk, shaking his head. He did not know what to do.

Discussion Questions

1 What is your opinion? Do parents have the right to choose teachers if there is room in the class?

2 If you disagree with the two principals at the meeting, how would you argue against them that parents have a legitimate right to select teachers?

3 If he believes this way, how should one of these principals handle the situation if he has a teacher whom very few parents want to choose? Should he forget his beliefs in this case and fill up the class anyway or decide that the teacher should be assigned some other duty or dismissed, if he has evidence of poor performance?

4 We often hear stories about the teacher whom no one liked and who was very demanding of students, but, years later, the same students say this was the best teacher they ever had. How does this fit into the discussion?

5 What is the assignment process in your school or in ones with which you are familiar?

PERFORMANCE OBJECTIVE

THE ADMINISTRATOR
—examines and considers the prevailing
  values of the diverse school community

Case Study 121

Martha Wyler had been raised in an affluent suburb of New Jersey and had attended the most prestigious universities in New England. Until her husband passed away, she really had had no desire to use her administrative licenses, but an untimely death mixed with overwhelming financial obligations forced her into the job market. She knew that an administrative position would give her the funds she needed and allow her to utilize her administrative expertise.

Reality quickly set in when she found that the only job available was an elementary principalship in an inner-city neighborhood that was overwhelmed with poverty and crime. Mrs. Wyler found that her prestigious background did not mesh with the surroundings in which she found herself, but she was not a quitter. She vowed that she would do all in her power to help the students and the families within her school district.

Mrs. Wyler met with her teachers and told them of her expectations for the students. She expected the students to be educated, but she also expected the teachers to be understanding and sympathetic to the plight of the students. She immediately set about trying to contact parents and establish some type of rapport between the school and the community. She asked that her teachers implement multicultural programs that would enhance the various cultures serviced by the school. She tried to explain to her staff the importance of recognizing cultural differences, as well as trying to enhance the standards of good American citizenship.

She wanted to establish the school as a safe haven and as a community meeting place for the residents. She actively sought input from parents, teachers, and community leaders. She enlisted their aid to design programs that would assist both the students and the adults who might also benefit from such programs.

Mrs. Wyler had many false starts and several times she found her trust had been betrayed. Quite often she went home frustrated but unbeaten. She knew that she and her staff were, little by little, making a difference.

Discussion Questions

1 Did the superintendent of the district do Mrs. Wyler a disservice by placing her in an inner-city elementary principalship?

2 Should educational administration courses include issues of culture and diversity?

3 How would you deal with an inner-city situation and maintain discipline as well as recognize cultural diversity?

4 How would you go about training your staff to be more sympathetic to and aware of community issues and values?

5 Are inner-city schools the only places where you would find diverse school and community values?

6 How do you deal with diversity and values that may be ''foreign'' to your own values?

7 What problems could be caused by the principal's proclivity to gamble for ''recreation''? If she can overcome the desire to gamble, could this experience be of any benefit to her in the school?

PERFORMANCE OBJECTIVE

THE ADMINISTRATOR
—expects that others in the school
  community will demonstrate integrity and
  exercise ethical behavior

Case Study 122

"I cannot believe that you and some of your fellow teachers actually gave the students answers to the proficiency test," said Mrs. Clark, the principal of Duke Senior High School. "Whatever possessed you to do such an unethical thing?"

Mr. Humes, the social studies teacher, shifted uncomfortably in his seat and looked down to avoid the principal's searing glare. "I only wanted our students to perform well on this test. You know how important these scores are to the district. And although I do not like to mention it, you have been pressuring all of us to improve our students' performance."

Mrs. Clark knew that Mr. Humes was at least partially right. The scores were considered by the state to be important benchmarks of the students' success or failure. It was also true that she had indicated on many occasions how imperative it was for the teachers to work with the students in areas covered by this proficiency test.

"I never suggested or implied that you or anyone else cheat on this exam. I wanted the students to do well, and I did say that our necks could be on the chopping block if the students performed unsatisfactorily. But at no time did I encourage you to cheat to get the job done. Mr. Humes, I have no other alternative but to invalidate the test scores and refer the matter to the central administration. We must all exercise ethical behaviors at all times. There is absolutely no excuse for what you and your fellow teachers did."

Discussion Questions

1 Do you think that the principal was in any way responsible for the action of the teachers?

2 How much do state mandates and unrealistic expectations influence the ethical and moral responsibilities of teachers and administrators?

3 Do you think that Mrs. Clark's decision to invalidate the scores was appropriate?

4 Do you agree with her decision to involve central administration with the disciplining of the teachers, or should she have handled the disciplining as an internal matter?

5 Do you think that ethics should be an issue that is discussed on a continual basis during inservice or professional development training sessions?

PERFORMANCE OBJECTIVE

THE ADMINISTRATOR
—opens the school to public scrutiny

Case Study 123

Jake Jackson had just taken over the principal's position after Mr. Robinson had been encouraged to take early retirement. When Jake came to the school district, he asked the superintendent and others why Mr. Robinson had left so suddenly. He was told that there had been several problems in the middle school building where Mr. Robinson had been principal.

First of all, many parents had questioned what had happened to money that had been raised by them to help the school. Mr. Robinson had taken the questioning personally and had told parents that the funds were safe and that nothing had happened to them. He felt insulted that anyone would want to know about the money. Eventually, it was found that Mr. Robinson had been correct. All the money was in a local bank account. However, parents were very upset that they had to wait several months for the answer, and some had begun to question Mr. Robinson's honesty when he would not reply to their questions.

In addition, a couple of parents wanted to see firsthand whether appropriate repairs had been made in the building where a couple of students had received minor injuries. Again, Mr. Robinson told the parents that the repairs had been made but that he did not allow parents to inspect the building, "or else everyone and their brother will want to come visit us every day about some complaint."

Finally, the local newspaper editor called the principal to ask him about these and other "public relations problems," as the reporter called them, at the school. The principal told the editor that he did not want any Watergate-type reporters coming into his building to find out about problems that did not exist. Upon investigation, Jake Jackson found that all repairs had been made as planned. In fact, Jake could not find any important problems at the school.

Discussion Questions

1 If it is true that Mr. Robinson had no real problems at the school, why would he hesitate in supplying answers to questions? Have you worked with people like this?

2 How could Mr. Robinson have reacted differently to the parents asking about the money? about the repairs? How might he have reacted to the editor?

3 Why do some administrators develop this "bunker" mentality? Is there something that could be done in university training or on-the-job training to help administrators avoid this problem?

4 What advice could you give to the new principal, Jake? What attitudes might he face initially from the public?

5 What specific steps could Jake take to bring back confidence in the school and the principalship, especially from the parents? from the media?

6 To what extent should schools be open to public scrutiny? Does the principal have to allow everyone to see or know everything?

7 What about access to the building by the public? Should parents be allowed to come into the building during the school day? Under what conditions? What about the media? What would you do if the television station called to say that they were coming at 1:00 P.M. to film students in the hallway or on the playground, to ask teachers some questions, or to film the area where students were injured in the building?

PERFORMANCE OBJECTIVE

THE ADMINISTRATOR
—fulfills legal and contractual obligations

Case Study 124

Mrs. Salinas, the principal of Elkhorn Middle School, was totally disgusted with the quality of milk that had been purchased for the school cafeteria. She was not satisfied with the packaging, nor did she like the fact that it was whole milk rather than the healthier low-fat milk. She phoned the milk distributor and voiced her dissatisfaction with the company. "If you do not rectify the situation, I will terminate your contract immediately," she told them.

Mr. Barker, the president of the company, listened attentively as he reached for the Elkhorn customer file that contained the school contract. "I am happy to help you and the students in any way I can, but I want you to understand that the contract specified whole milk in plastic pouches rather than in the traditional cartons. I think, Mrs. Salinas, that you had better read your contract before you threaten us."

After her anger subsided, Mrs. Salinas realized that Mr. Barker was correct. She and the school had a contractual obligation with the milk distributor, and their product and service were exactly as had been specified. She knew she had three avenues from which to choose: terminate the contract and face a possible lawsuit, accept the contract for the remainder of its term and then use another distributor, or negotiate with Mr. Barker to revise the contract.

Discussion Questions

1 How important are contractual obligations to a principal when the welfare of the students is in question?

2 Should Mrs. Salinas have been more cognizant of the contract before it was initiated?

3 Do you think that Mrs. Salinas was correct in threatening to terminate the contract with Mr. Barker?

4 Do you believe that Mr. Barker would have sued Mrs. Salinas and the school for breach of contract?

5 How legally binding are contracts?

6 What are the moral and ethical solutions to contractual obligations?

7 Which of the three options do you believe Mrs. Salinas chose? Give reasons for your choice.

8 Should Mrs. Salinas have contacted someone else in the district before calling the milk company? If so, whom?

9 Most legal contracts are made at the board/superintendent level. What contractual obligations would Mrs. Salinas encounter at the school level, even though she may not have been involved in the legal decision?

PERFORMANCE OBJECTIVE

THE ADMINISTRATOR
—applies laws and procedures fairly, wisely, and considerately

Case Study 125

The new principal wants to get off to a strong start at school and considers the following potential problems that teachers have expressed concerns about.

- Students with two or more unauthorized absences, class cuts, should be penalized. Why not bar these students from field trips or other special activities in those classes?
- Students on inside, in-school, suspension are required to work on assignments from each of their classes. Should they get only partial credit for these, since they are suspended? Should a certain percentage be fixed at, say, 70% maximum allowable credit?
- Participation in the Campus to Community Service Project includes work as a hospital volunteer; clean up and restoration of Cedar Lake; participation in the community fall festival, including band concerts and parades, booths, and the pancake breakfast;

and a variety of other alternatives. Why not encourage participation by allowing participating students to receive an extra credit grade in a class of their choice?

- Students often do not attend meetings with their counselors, especially if they are having difficulties. Others cut required quiet study halls. Since attendance point totals are kept toward special recognition certificates and great prizes, including certificates for free pizzas at the end of the school year, for example, should students forfeit attendance points if they fail to attend counselor meetings or study halls? Might an alternative be offered to students, such as a choice of "making up" the attendance day, forfeiting one or more special all-school assembly days or Sports Day held during the year?

- Students always attend the school dances, but many leave and then try to get back into the dance. Should a new rule be instituted stating that once you leave, you cannot return to the dance?

- Displays of unsportsmanlike conduct (booing the other team or coach; shouting out to referees, from the bench or the stands; baiting someone on the opposing team or physically challenging any other student present at the sports event, etc.) occur in almost every athletic contest, in one form or another. Why not suspend from attendance or participation any student who is caught violating the school's "Good Sportsmanship Code"? One might extend the penalty for the rest of the school year, including all sports events.

- Students who are truant (unauthorized absence) are required to complete the work assigned in each of their classes. But should they be allowed no credit for the work? Instead, might the assignments completed be placed in their permanent files with a full record of the truancy?

Discussion Questions

1 Comment on each of the situations/problems noted above, paying particular attention to the effect each has on students' academic efforts. Amend the consequence that the principal considers for

each situation if you think that is appropriate—or pose a more suitable alternative for the problem.

2 What advice would you give to this new principal whose intention is to present a strong front and hold students accountable as he makes them responsible for all their choices and actions?

3 What guidelines for effective decision-making (a list of 10 or 12 rules or suggestions, clear but concise working principles) can lead administrators to initiate fair and prudent policy and procedural changes? For example: Talk to student, ascertain motives, or treat others as you would wish your son or daughter to be treated.

4 Do most school rules and regulations deter infractions? In what cases will rules actually encourage, if not provoke, infringement or misbehaviors?

5 How does a school leader create a balance when promulgating rules and regulations? Can rules be fair but also firm? consistent but consequential? adapted to the individual case but applicable to all students?

CHAPTER 8

Standard 6 Case Studies

A school administrator is an educational leader who promotes the success of all students by understanding, responding to, and influencing the larger political, social, economic, legal, and cultural context.

PERFORMANCE OBJECTIVE

THE ADMINISTRATOR FACILITATES
PROCESSES AND ENGAGES IN
ACTIVITIES ENSURING THAT
—The environment in which schools operate
is influenced on behalf of students and
their families.

Case Study 126

The principal considers some of the most troubling problems that may confront students to include failure to stay in school and graduate, succumbing to gang influences, experimenting with or dealing in controlled substances, and engaging in unprotected sexual activity and/or promiscuity.

Caveat: The format here will be different from most case studies throughout this text, since the emphasis shifts to the principal recognizing and responding to problems.

Discussion Questions

1 How might a principal gauge that any or all of these are problems for district students? What is involved in identifying the nature and extent of problems like those listed above?

For example, some administrators follow certain prescribed criteria, based on their own experience, in determining whether an issue, event, or situation is a problem. The ''criteria'' one principal might use include these considerations:

- The issue, event, or situation is serious and important; it may have legal implications or ramifications.
- It may influence or affect more than a few students in school.
- Several people have contacted the main office with concerns about it.
- School policies and regulations currently do not cover it.
- Administrators in other districts have identified this as a concern to them.

2 How does one determine the school's responsibility in terms of identified problems? What might be possible alternative strategies to pursue in dealing with each problem?

3 What is the community's role in responding to any or all of these problems, if they, in fact, do exist? How might parent/guardians be drawn in to help? What roles might they assume?

4 What steps might a principal take to solve each of the problems if they do exist? Consider appropriate measures if each problem is recent, on-going, severe, or at crisis level.

Comments

Reference: *The Knowledge Base in Educational Administration: Multiple Perspectives,* eds. Robert Donmoyer, Michael Imber, and James Joseph Scheurich (Albany: State University of New York Press, 1995). Some scholars argue that preparation of school administrators might well include identifying, assessing, and resolving problems.

PERFORMANCE OBJECTIVE

THE ADMINISTRATOR FACILITATES
PROCESSES AND ENGAGES IN
ACTIVITIES ENSURING THAT
—The environment in which schools operate
 is influenced on behalf of students and
 their families.

Case Study 127

The site-based management team of Robertson High School was in its third hour of meeting when Mrs. Salazar, the principal, interrupted an argument that seemed to dominate the meeting. Mrs. Salazar tried to maintain calmness and decorum on the surface, but inside she was seething with anger and frustration. This anger was directed at several members of the site-based team whose mission was to serve as school facilitators. These people—teachers, parents, and business owners—were supposed to offer help and guidance to the overall functioning of Robertson High School. But Mrs. Salazar soon understood that very few of the members' agendas really dealt with the needs of the students and the community.

The business owners were there simply to seek new markets for their products. They looked upon the students and the community as a captive audience, and they hoped to fill their own pockets at the expense of the students and their parents. Several of the community members were out of touch with the demographics and the social needs of the school. Even worse, the teachers on the site-based management team were out of touch with the academic needs of the Robertson High School students. As a result, the meetings were, more often than not, unproductive—even counterproductive—and very contentious. Arguments were becoming the norm.

"Ladies and gentlemen, this action must cease," Mrs. Salazar said as she glared at the faces around the library table. "We are here to guide this school and to try and make it a better place for our students. What we do here at Robertson will have an effect on the community. Our school can become a resource for the community and a source of pride for all of us. I urge you to stop this bickering and to consider the welfare of the students."

"We are trying," said Mrs. Sneed, a parent whose daughter had always been in the top ten percent of her class. "We do want all of the students at Robertson to be high achievers, just like my daughter, Sheila."

Mrs. Salazar fought the urge to roll her eyes back in her head as she managed to say, "Thank you, Mrs. Sneed. Unfortunately, not all of our students are blessed with Sheila's academic abilities. Nor are all of our students blessed by having parents who have been as successful as you and your husband.''

''We do want what is best for the students,'' said Mr. Trevino, the math teacher. Often Trevino was the only sane voice of reason on the site-based management team. ''Let's remember that we are dealing with many different types of students here at Robertson. We have to look out for the interests of not only the very best, but also the neediest— of which there are many. Let's turn our attention to these students and, possibly, their families.''

Mrs. Salazar breathed a silent prayer of thanks for having Mr. Trevino on the team. ''I concur with Mr. Trevino. We must remember the populations with which we deal and try our best to address *all* of our students' needs.''

Discussion Questions

1 What is the function of the site-based management team?
2 What is the principal's role in dealing with a site-based management team?
3 Do you think Mrs. Salazar let the meeting deteriorate too far?
4 What are the ethical ramifications of business persons serving on site-based management teams?
5 Was Mr. Trevino correct in his assessment of dealing with the needs of the entire school population?
6 How would you have reacted to Mrs. Sneed if you were the principal of Robertson High School?
7 What steps can the meeting's participants take to address some of the needs of its diverse school populace? All eventually agree that Robertson students must have as good a high school education as possible, and that graduates must be prepared for future education or successful employment.
8 Provide several examples of how school districts have changed the environment in which they operate on behalf of students and their families. One district, for example, holds a series of evening open meetings and invites all parent/guardians. The six-part series deals with: (1) students' success in academics, (2) focusing on available community resources, (3) explaining the wide range of postgraduate

choices available for students, (4) offering work-study options, (5) utilizing the counseling department services, and (6) tutorial and mentoring available.

PERFORMANCE OBJECTIVE

THE ADMINISTRATOR FACILITATES
PROCESSES AND ENGAGES IN
ACTIVITIES ENSURING THAT
—Communication occurs among the school
community concerning trends, issues, and
potential changes in the environment in
which schools operate.

Case Study 128

A traditional institution with strong community support, Central High School is highly regarded. However, the neighborhood surrounding the school has changed markedly in the last five years. During this period, diverse groups have sought a better standard of living, safer streets, better schools, and additional employment opportunities. Thus, many new residents have chosen the area surrounding Central High School as a good place to live and work. The changing community is reflected in current census data that reveal almost 20% of the population is now non-white. Census data have been discussed informally among Chamber of Commerce members, Rotary, and other key community organizations. Yet, the high school board of education, if not administrators, seeks to maintain the school's traditions from the past; they feel that the district's reputation is at stake.

Discussion Questions

1 How might administrators ascertain that there are problems with their commitment to the past and to the school's traditions and reputation? What signs or "symptoms" indicate problems? Can a changing school community be encouraged to embrace the school's traditions? In addition, what negative results ought administrators,

faculty, and staff anticipate in view of this pull toward the past and a school's traditions?

2 How does a school like Central High maintain traditions and its enviable reputation and also change enough to welcome, if not accommodate, new members of the school community?

3 What steps might district leaders choose to create awareness of, sensitivity to, and harmony among all members of the Central High School community? Community action groups and social service agencies, for example, might be willing to offer suggestions, programs, and lists of speaker/experts who specialize in this and related topics.

4 Offer Central High School's board of education a "white paper" outline directed to the topic "Prospectus for Change." What headings might appear in this overview? Where might a committee interested in evolving such a document obtain research on the efforts of other districts to accommodate changing communities, changing schools?

Comments

Change is much more the rule than the exception in life; note how the global marketplace has become a contemporary reality, for example. Technology makes our connection to an international network as close as the nearest computer. Many school districts accommodate a variety of changes, in programs and services, in new ways of educating students, and in the philosophy governing a school's mission and vision. On the level of operating an effective and efficient school program, however, things can get complicated. One high school staff, for example, noted racial divisions in extracurricular activities. Students of ethnic diversity joined sports squads, especially soccer and football teams, but were absent from theater or speech activities. A new Culture Club had student members from only one cultural group. Faculty and administrators debated how they might encourage all students to take advantage of the many opportunities to participate in school activities, both academic and nonacademic. Did they exceed appropriate expectations in their concern? How does a district adjust to a changing community and serve all members of the student body? How does a group of administrators encourage everyone interested in education to work toward a stronger school?

PERFORMANCE OBJECTIVE

THE ADMINISTRATOR FACILITATES
PROCESSES AND ENGAGES IN
ACTIVITIES ENSURING THAT
—There is ongoing dialogue with
   representatives of diverse community
   groups.

Case Study 129

The superintendent of District 203 receives a call from the town business council when a feature article appears in the local newspaper. A reporter attended the recent board meeting and wrote about reopening discussions on the subject of open campus. Students are petitioning for a change in school rules that will require their attendance only for scheduled classes. "You know what happened when we had open campus years ago," the council representative complains. "Students were in all of our stores downtown, some even annoying customers. Even the bus drivers couldn't get a table at Marlowe's cafe in the morning for all the kids!"

The next call is from an irate homeowner on Potter Road across from the upper-division building. Students are trampling through her flower beds when they leave school in the afternoon; they cut right across the lawns, too.

At day's end, yet another community member calls to alert the superintendent to the school's resurfaced track facing Dempster Street. "What are all your teachers doing taking exercise on the track?" the caller asks. "We pay their salaries—and we don't pay them to exercise on school time. Some of them are running at noon!" Sure enough, the superintendent swivels in his chair and sees five or six teachers running around the track. It is 3:35 P.M.

Discussion Questions

1 Are these complaints about students and teachers legitimate grievances? How should a superintendent respond to the callers, or are they just old "fussbudgets" with nothing better to do?

2 A school is a community resource, and, as such, is open to a variety of community programs and adult evening courses. The superintendent is struck by some callers' expectations, as though the community can have a say in the open campus policy. Next they'll want to have their say on programs and courses offered. Who has priority here?

3 The principal now has two points of view to consider regarding open campus: students petitioning and the local business council. Is compromise possible when views are so divergent? How might parent/guardians view the open campus privilege? Might other community people support the business owners?

Comments

Keeping the dialogue active between a school district and its community is desirable, if not necessary. School partnerships begin with good public relations efforts; schools and community groups have a lot to offer one another. Maintaining strong ties with people in the school's immediate locale almost always guarantees their support when needed for the future. School leaders have an obligation to articulate their commitment to educating young people and fulfilling a role as a resource. Students have responsibilities to uphold in the school community and in the neighborhoods that circle their building.

PERFORMANCE OBJECTIVE

THE ADMINISTRATOR FACILITATES
PROCESSES AND ENGAGES IN
ACTIVITIES ENSURING THAT
—The school community works within the
  framework of policies, laws, and regulations
  enacted by local, state, and federal
  authorities.

Case Study 130

Mr. Swanson, the principal of Montclair Middle School, was just on his way to a ball game when the telephone rang. His first impulse was to simply close the door and ignore it. However, he reluctantly moved to the secretary's desk where he picked up the telephone only to be greeted by a sobbing voice on the other end.

"Is this the principal?" asked a distraught woman.

"Yes, it is. Who is this and how may I help you?"

"I am Randy Mathis's mother. I am glad I am able to speak with you about Randy and the problems we are having, Mr. Swanson."

Mr. Swanson pulled out the secretary's chair and sat down. He sensed that this woman had problems and that the ball game would have to wait.

"I have a favor to ask, Mr. Swanson. I need your permission to take Randy to Florida for a month to six weeks. We are going to visit my parents down there because my husband and I are having problems and I need to get away."

"Mrs. Mathis," Mr. Swanson began, "I cannot give you permission to take your child out of school for that length of time. The state law says that there is a mandatory attendance requirement until a child reaches the age of 16. Randy would miss a tremendous amount of classroom work which would also involve a great deal of classroom participation."

"Mr. Swanson, I do not want to go into details about the relationship between my husband and me. Believe me, I need to get away and I cannot leave my son alone with my husband."

"Mrs. Mathis, I certainly sympathize with your situation; however, I am an officer of the state and I must enforce the laws as they pertain to education. I cannot give you permission to take your son out of school for four to six weeks. I do not have that authority. Perhaps we could speak with his teachers and explain the situation; they might be willing to provide advanced assignments for Randy. Upon his return, those assignments could be graded by the participating teachers. It will be up to them to decide if they will be willing to cooperate with you."

Discussion Questions

1 How would you have reacted to Mrs. Mathis's request if you were the principal of the school?

2 Was Mr. Swanson fair in his dealings with Mrs. Mathis?

3 Did Mr. Swanson assume the proper responsibility for the attendance of the students?

4 Would you adhere to the letter of the law when it came to enforcing all local, state, and federal laws and mandates?

5 Would you have taken Mrs. Mathis at her word, or would you have done further investigation before rendering a judgment?

6 Should Mr. Swanson involve the teachers in this situation?

7 Should Mr. Swanson try to find out more about the "problem," or is it not his business?

PERFORMANCE OBJECTIVE

THE ADMINISTRATOR FACILITATES
PROCESSES AND ENGAGES IN
ACTIVITIES ENSURING THAT
—Public policy is shaped to provide quality
  education for students.

Case Study 131

Superintendent Mark Andrews received a call from a state official asking him if he would be willing to testify before a legislative committee, detailing his views on school funding and how the current state formula and proposed state formula would affect his school district. The superintendent had planned to attend another local area meeting that day, but he could send another administrator and go to the state committee meeting. He did have strong feelings about state funding of education and how it would affect his students in the future. But he also wondered whether his testimony would make any difference.

Discussion Questions

1 How should Mr. Andrews weigh his decision about attending a local meeting where he was sure he would have an effect or attending this state meeting where he did not know what effect his speaking would have?

2 Assume that Mr. Andrews accepted the invitation to go to the state committee. How should he prepare? How long should he speak? Should he bring a prepared paper? If so, should he read the paper? How should he address the committee? How can he find the right answers to these questions so he does not have to guess the correct protocol?

3 What difference, if any, does it make for him to speak to the committee if they are hearing from other people as well?

4 Do legislative members and staff listen to these speakers? Do these speakers influence their actions, votes, and public policy?

5 Had Mr. Andrews not been invited, how could he have made his opinion heard? Does it make any difference for a local school superintendent to write any legislators?

6 Are there ways for Mr. Andrews to establish good relations with the local legislators prior to asking for anything?

PERFORMANCE OBJECTIVE

THE ADMINISTRATOR FACILITATES
PROCESSES AND ENGAGES IN
ACTIVITIES ENSURING THAT
—Public policy is shaped to provide quality
  education for students.

Case Study 132

Two days after Mr. Andrews addressed the state legislative committee on school funding, his board of education had its regular monthly meeting. Under "New Business," superintendent Andrews spoke to the board. "Last week I was asked to address a state legislative committee about how our schools are funded. I spoke to the committee and presented them with a written copy of my comments. I enclosed a copy of that paper in your board packet for you to see. It is very important that we—and I mean the people attending this meeting, too—write and speak to our legislators and tell them how we feel about this new proposed school funding formula. It will make a difference in the amount of money this district will get if it is enacted into law. We need to do the best that we can for our students. I have left copies of my comments and a list of the legislators' addresses on that table for those in the audience.''

"The next item on the agenda is appropriate since it involves funding my recommendation to try a new program on a pilot basis to see if it works: We propose to try to improve mathematics and English using this configuration of staff on a trial basis. Note that it only costs about $3,000. You have received the details in your packet.''

"Mr. Andrews,'' said board member Donald Nowak, ''I am not sure about this new program or whether it will work, but you also have recommended that we purchase new band uniforms for $8,000. We really need those uniforms. I move that we table the proposal on the new program and purchase the new uniforms.''

Discussion Questions

1 Was it a good idea for Mr. Andrews to tell the board about his talk to the state committee? to give copies to the public? to ask the public to contact their legislators?

2 Is the superintendent becoming too involved in politics? What should be the role of the superintendent in politics?

3 What is your reaction to Mr. Nowak's motion?

4 More importantly, how should Mr. Andrews react to Mr. Nowak? If you were another board member, what would you say?

Comments

This case study did actually happen at a board meeting. The superintendent reacted by telling the board that the public might question the board's priorities if they approved band uniforms and did not approve the academic program. The board voted to approve Mr. Nowak's motion. Later, board members demanded that Mr. Andrews apologize to the board publicly for insulting them. If you were Mr. Andrews, how would you react to the board?

PERFORMANCE OBJECTIVE

THE ADMINISTRATOR FACILITATES
PROCESSES AND ENGAGES IN
ACTIVITIES ENSURING THAT
—Lines of communication are developed with
decision-makers outside the school
community.

Case Study 133

Significant decision-makers outside the school community include:

- local community college and technical institute administrators and program directors
- local politicians
- the real estate community
- community service board and community service organizations
- park district administrators and program directors
- the public library board and administrators
- city finance department
- the Chamber of Commerce
- the Adolescent Social Service Center
- the Church Alliance Council

Discussion Questions

1 Suggest what lines of communication (monthly meetings? workshops or special interest activities? yearly retreats?) may be pursued with the above groups. Are any groups to be considered more important than the others?

2 How can each group or organization benefit students, school, and the school program—directly or indirectly? What impact is possible in view of each listed?

3 Describe the impact or influence of several of the above listed that you, personally, know of in terms of students, schools, and school programs.

4 Suggest 5–10 other decision-makers outside the school community who can be important in terms of the school program and students'

success. Use your own knowledge of the community in which your school is located.

Comments

Reform efforts recognize the importance of all stakeholders in the educational programs and services provided by a school district. Community organizations are among the stakeholders. For example, park districts offer opportunities that include special workshops, sports at all levels, skills development, etc. These target a range of supplementary programs that help students. Administrators and counselors might offer to serve on park district boards, which could also include student representatives. Program decisions might include their views. In this case, park districts can offer programs and services that schools do not offer.

About the Authors

Dr. William L. Sharp is Associate Dean of the College of Education at Southern Illinois University at Carbondale and a Professor in the Department of Educational Administration and Higher Education. Prior to these positions, he was an Associate Professor at the University of Akron, a high school mathematics teacher, an administrator, and a school superintendent in Indiana and Illinois. During his superintendencies, *Executive Educator* selected him as one of the top 100 superintendents in the country. He has an A.B. in mathematics and an M.S. in secondary education from Indiana University, a graduate Diploma of Education from Durham University in England, where he was a Durham Scholar, and a Ph.D. from Northwestern University. He has had many articles published in education journals, *The New York Times*, and the *Cleveland Plain Dealer*. His first book, *Collective Bargaining in the Public Schools*, was published by Brown and Benchmark. The next two books, *The Principal as School Manager* and *The School Superintendent: The Profession and the Person*, co-authored with Dr. Walter, were published by Technomic Publishing.

Dr. James K. Walter is Associate Professor of Educational Administration at Texas A&M at Corpus Christi. Prior to that, he was

Program Coordinator of Educational Administration at Salem State College, Massachusetts, after serving as superintendent at Dudley Charlton Regional School District in Massachusetts. Prior to this superintendency, he was an Associate Superintendent in Ohio, an Assistant Professor at the University of Akron, and an adjunct professor at Ashland University, Ohio, and at Indiana University. A native of Kokomo, he received his B.S. in English education from Indiana University and his M.A.E. and Ed.D. in school administration from Ball State University. With his wealth of knowledge in many areas, he has authored numerous articles and essays for professional books and journals. He is the author of the Phi Delta Kappa booklet, *The Elementary Principal as Fiscal Manager*, and the co-author of *The Principal as School Manager* and *The School Superintendent: The Profession and the Person* with Dr. Sharp. He and his wife, Deborah, have two children, Zachary and Andrea.

Helen M. Sharp is a professional writer, educational consultant, and motivational speaker. She has extensive experience writing in business and industrial settings. A career educator with administrative licenses, she has contributed over 50 articles to state and national educational publications. She is also a regular reviewer for the *NASSP Bulletin*. With a Master of Arts degree in English from Marquette University and 33 additional hours of study in English at the Ph.D. level, she has taught middle school and secondary English as well as community college and university courses in advanced composition, business writing, technical writing, and professional development. As a consultant with her husband, Dr. Sharp, she conducts workshops for board members, administrators, professional and noncertificated school staff members. The Sharps specialize in practical solutions to educational problems. An experienced convention and conference speaker, she motivates audiences with dynamic energy and enthusiasm. A creative writer, she has penned many serious as well as humorous columns for newspapers. Her work has been featured in *Akron* magazine, and she has had an entry in the acclaimed gender studies collection, *I Am Beautiful*. Current projects include a book project and a research study of school communications.

Index

The following index lists some of the topics covered in the case studies. The number after each category is the number of the **case study**, not the page number.